The Serenity Solution: Mastering Happiness through Meditation

By: Richard D. Krause

While every precaution has been taken in the preparation of this book, the publisher assumes no responsibility for errors or omissions, or for damages resulting from the use of the information contained herein.

THE SERENITY SOLUTION: MASTERING HAPPINESS THROUGH MEDITATION

First edition. November 2, 2023.

Copyright © 2023 Richard D. Krause.

ISBN: 979-8223101918

Written by Richard D. Krause.

Also by Richard D. Krause

The Elderly Trap: Uncovering Scams and Reclaiming Security in the
Golden Years.
Ignite Your Motivation and Achieve Your Dreams
The Art of Persoal Mastery: A Roadmap to Success and Fulfillment
The Serenity Solution: Mastering Happiness through Meditation

Table of Contents

This work is dedicated to my two wonderful daughters, Kristina and Erica. One dynamic the other chaotic. May the reading of this book help and guide you on your continued journey down the path of life.

I love you!

Introduction: Embarking on a Journey of Inner Transformation

In the hustle and bustle of our modern world, where our minds are perpetually bombarded with information, responsibilities, and distractions, finding a moment of peace and tranquility can seem like an elusive dream. The demands of daily life can leave us feeling stressed, anxious, and disconnected from our true selves. It's in this whirlwind of chaos that the ancient practice of meditation emerges as a guiding light, a way to rediscover harmony, purpose, and lasting happiness.

Welcome to "*The Serenity Solution: Mastering Happiness through Meditation*," your gateway to a profound and transformative journey of self-discovery. In the pages that follow, we will explore the art and science of meditation, unlocking its secrets and demystifying its practice. Whether you are entirely new to meditation or have dabbled in it before, this book is designed to be your trusted companion on this path.

Why Meditate?

YOU MIGHT BE WONDERING, "Why should I start meditating?" The answer is simple yet profound: meditation holds the key to unlocking the door to inner peace, self-awareness, and enduring happiness. It offers a sanctuary of stillness amidst life's storms, a place where you can connect with your deepest self and navigate the challenges of existence with grace and resilience.

Throughout the chapters of this book, we will delve into various meditation techniques, each with its unique approach to fostering mindfulness, compassion, and mental clarity. You will discover the power of mindfulness meditation, the healing potential of loving-kindness meditation, the soothing effects of body scan meditation, and the transformative nature of mantra meditation, among others.

Your Journey Begins Here

THIS BOOK IS DESIGNED with you, the beginner, in mind. We will start with the basics, guiding you through the process of establishing a meditation practice that suits your lifestyle and needs. You will learn how to create a sacred meditation space, how to sit comfortably, and how to breathe mindfully.

As we progress, you will explore the different forms of meditation, giving you the opportunity to choose the one that resonates most with you. Guided by our expert guidance, you'll embark on a journey of self-awareness, emotional balance, and personal growth.

Overcoming Challenges

MEDITATION IS NOT WITHOUT its challenges. The wandering mind, impatience, and life's inevitable distractions can deter even the most dedicated practitioners. We'll address these common obstacles head-on, offering strategies to help you overcome them and stay committed to your practice.

A Lifelong Adventure

"The Serenity Solution: Mastering Happiness through Meditation" is not just a book; it's an invitation to embark on a lifelong adventure. Whether your goal is to reduce stress, improve concentration, find inner peace, or simply explore the depths of your consciousness, meditation is a path that will continue to unfold before you, offering new insights and rewards at every turn.

Your journey of self-discovery and transformation begins now. So, turn the page, take a deep breath, and let's begin this extraordinary exploration of meditation, happiness, and the boundless potential that resides within you. Together, we will unlock the door to a world of inner peace, clarity, and joy.

Chapter 1: Introduction to Meditation

In the ceaseless rhythm of our hectic lives, where time evaporates like dew in the morning sun, there lies an ancient practice, a serene refuge that promises a profound transformation—a practice known as meditation. So, what is this mystical art of meditation, and why are people raving about its life-altering effects?

Imagine, if you will, a realm beyond the cacophony of your daily existence, where the incessant chatter of the mind gives way to a soothing symphony of calmness. Meditation is not just a practice; it's an odyssey into the depths of your own consciousness, a journey that holds the potential to redefine the very fabric of your being.

In the heart of this exploration is the quest for happiness, a pursuit so universal and yet so elusive. You might be pondering, "How can simply being happy be the key to happiness?" It's a perplexing notion; one that challenges the conventional wisdom that happiness is a reaction to external circumstances. But here's the paradox: happiness, in its purest form, is not circumstantial; it's a state of being that emerges from within.

Now, let's dispel a common notion, achieving happiness is not a whimsical feat reserved for a chosen few. It's not about plastering a smile on your face and pretending all is well, oblivious to the struggles and tragedies life inevitably throws at you. Happiness, in the realm of meditation, is a nuanced dance with your inner self, a dance that acknowledges the storms while finding solace in the stillness within.

You might be asking, "How do I even begin to be happy? Can I really train my mind to be happy more often than not?" These are questions that echo in the minds of many, and the answer lies in a pause, a pause that leads us to the heart of meditation.

The Essence of Meditation Unveiled

MEDITATION IS NOT A mystical ritual confined to mountaintop gurus or those seeking enlightenment in secluded monasteries. It's a practice available to anyone willing to take a moment, breathe, and journey inward. Picture this: you, amidst the chaos, pressing the pause button on life's incessant demands, finding a serene spot within yourself.

Let's unravel the layers. Meditation is not a one-size-fits-all endeavor. It's a diverse landscape with various techniques, each offering a unique gateway to inner peace. Close your eyes, take a deep breath, and imagine the possibilities, mindfulness meditation, where you embrace the present moment; loving-kindness meditation, where compassion becomes a guiding force; and mantra meditation, where the rhythmic chant of words leads you to a tranquil state.

But Why Meditate?

"WHY SHOULD I DIVE INTO the world of meditation?" you might wonder. The answer, my friend, is rooted in the chaos we call life. Amidst the hustle and bustle, meditation is your anchor. It's the space where you detach from the noise and reconnect with the essence of your being. Picture a turbulent ocean; meditation is the still point at its center.

Through the upcoming chapters, we'll venture into the practicalities, explore the diverse techniques, and discover how even a few minutes a day can be a lifeline in the storm. But first, let's acknowledge the skepticism that may linger. In a world fixated on tangible outcomes and immediate gratification, the concept of finding happiness within seems almost too surreal, too counterintuitive.

The Skeptic's Dilemma

SO, LET'S ADDRESS THE elephant in the room, skepticism. You might find this whole idea of meditation, happiness, and the intertwining of the two a tad ludicrous. And that's perfectly okay. Before you dismiss it outright, let's embark on a shared journey of curiosity. Pause, reflect, and ask yourself, "What if?" What if, hidden within the stillness of meditation, lies a reservoir of joy waiting to be tapped?

As we navigate through the chapters ahead, be open to the possibility that this practice, once considered esoteric, might just be the missing piece in your pursuit of happiness. Don't fret; skepticism is a passenger we all carry at some point. It's the questioning mind seeking proof, and we'll honor it by unraveling the practical, tangible benefits meditation can bring to your life.

In Conclusion: A Pause, A Breath, A Beginning

IN THE VAST TAPESTRY of life, where every thread weaves a unique story, meditation is your invitation to craft a narrative of happiness. This isn't a magical incantation promising instant bliss; it's a pragmatic exploration, a journey where you are both the traveler and the destination.

So, dear reader, take a deep breath, exhale the doubts, and let's venture into the realm of meditation together. Chapter by chapter, breath by breath, we'll unravel the mysteries, dispel the myths, and discover the transformative power that awaits within the folds of a mindful pause. The journey begins now, with a simple act, a pause, a breath, a beginning.

Chapter 2: Why Start Meditating?

In the tapestry of existence, where each thread is woven with moments of joy, challenges, and the mundane, the quest for happiness emerges as a universal yearning. As we stand at the crossroads of our lives, it's only natural to ponder: Why start meditating? What is the allure that draws people into the gentle embrace of this ancient practice, and why is it touted as a transformative journey worth embarking upon?

The Heart's Whisper: Craving for Fulfillment

IN THE BUSTLING SYMPHONY of our daily lives, the heart often whispers, seeking something more profound than the transient highs and lows. The craving for fulfillment, for a sense of purpose that transcends the superficial, is a common chord that resonates within each of us. This craving, this yearning for a deeper connection with life, is the first whisper that leads many to the doorstep of meditation.

Picture this: You, amidst the chaos, sensing an unspoken calling to explore the corridors of your inner world. This calling, often drowned by the noise of deadlines and obligations, becomes a beacon when we pause and listen. Meditation is the art of listening to that inner whisper, a compass guiding you towards a life rich in meaning and joy.

The Elusive Pursuit of Happiness

HAPPINESS, THAT ELUSIVE butterfly, flits just beyond our grasp in the cacophony of our pursuit. We find ourselves entangled in the web of achievements, relationships, and societal expectations, hoping that one day; we'll catch that elusive creature and hold it close. But here's the paradox: happiness, when sought externally, slips through our fingers like fine sand.

Meditation invites us to reframe our approach. It beckons us to turn our gaze inward, to explore the vast landscapes of our consciousness. Here, in the quietude of self-reflection, we find that the key to lasting happiness isn't a treasure to be sought; it's a latent power residing within.

The Pull of the Present Moment

IN A WORLD FIXATED on the past and the future, the present moment often slips away, a fleeting whisper lost in the winds of time. But what if the secret to happiness lies in the present, in fully experiencing and appreciating the now? This is where meditation unfurls its magic.

Mindfulness meditation, a cornerstone of the meditative journey, teaches us to be present without judgment. It's not about erasing the past or fretting about the future; it's about relishing the sweetness of the present. As we become attuned to the rhythm of our breath, the symphony of the present moment plays, and happiness is not a distant goal but a companion in our journey.

The Science of Serotonin and Endorphins

NOW, LET'S DIVE INTO the fascinating world of neuroscience. The brain, that intricate web of neurons and synapses, holds the key to understanding why meditation is more than just a subjective experience, it's a biochemical dance within.

When we meditate, the brain releases a cascade of neurotransmitters, including serotonin and endorphins, our body's natural mood enhancers. These chemicals, often dubbed the "happiness hormones," not only elevate our mood but also contribute to an overall sense of well-being. So, meditation is not just a spiritual sojourn; it's a dance of chemicals that harmonize to create a symphony of joy within.

Untangling the Web of Stress

STRESS, THAT EVER-PRESENT shadow, looms over our lives like a storm cloud. The demands of work, relationships, and the perpetual pursuit of more can cast a shadow over the sunniest of days. Meditation, like a gentle breeze, has the power to disperse this cloud, revealing the clarity that lies beyond.

In the sanctuary of meditation, the body's stress response undergoes a profound transformation. The parasympathetic nervous system, responsible for the "rest and digest" mode, takes center stage. As you breathe, as you delve into the meditative space, the body unwinds, and the web of stress begins to loosen its grip.

The Symphony of Self-Discovery

WHY START MEDITATING? Because it's not just a practice; it's an odyssey into self-discovery. In the silence between breaths, in the stillness of your mind, you encounter facets of yourself that often remain veiled in the daily hustle. Meditation is a journey where you become the explorer, navigating the labyrinth of your thoughts and emotions.

As you delve into mindfulness, you peel back the layers of conditioned responses, societal expectations, and self-imposed limitations. Here, in the crucible of self-awareness, you discover the power to shape your narrative, to choose happiness not as a reaction but as a conscious decision.

The Allure of Lasting Happiness

SO, WHY START MEDITATING? Because it's an invitation to lasting happiness. In the world of instant gratification, the idea of a practice that unfolds its gifts gradually might seem perplexing. Yet, therein lies the beauty, the slow bloom of a flower, the gradual dawn of a new day.

Happiness, through meditation, is not a fleeting moment but a state of being. It's the art of weaving contentment into the fabric of your life, regardless of external circumstances. It's the allure of a joy that doesn't waver with the tides of fortune but stands firm in the sanctuary of your own consciousness.

In the journey ahead, we'll explore the practicalities, delve into various meditation techniques, and unveil the myriad ways this ancient practice can reshape the contours of your life. So, as we stand at the threshold of this exploration, take a deep breath, and ponder: What if the pursuit of happiness isn't a chase but a homecoming to the serenity within? The journey has just begun.

Chapter 3: Getting Started

In the hustle of our everyday lives, where time slips through our fingers like grains of sand, the idea of finding a moment for oneself might seem like a whimsical dream. But imagine this: a tranquil sanctuary within your own space, a pause in the relentless dance of life. That's the essence of getting started with meditation, a practice not confined to mountain retreats or sacred temples but accessible to you, right here, right now.

Creating Your Meditation Space: A Haven of Tranquility

THE FIRST STEP IN THIS journey is crafting a haven, your personal meditation space. Picture this space not as a grandiose shrine but as a cozy nook where serenity wraps around you like a warm embrace. It could be a corner of your living room, a spot by the window, or even a cushion on the floor.

Consider the lighting, soft, gentle, inviting. Perhaps a candle flickering in the corner or the warm glow of a Himalayan salt lamp. Add a touch of nature, a potted plant or a vase of fresh flowers. This is your refuge, a place where the outside noise fades, and you step into a world of inner quietude.

The Art of Sitting Comfortably: Aligning Body and Mind

NOW THAT YOUR SANCTUARY is set, let's talk about the art of sitting comfortably. Contrary to the images of yogis contorted into pretzel shapes, meditation is not about pushing your body to extremes. It's about finding a posture that allows you to sit comfortably for the duration of your practice.

Begin by sitting on a cushion or a chair with your back straight. Feel the connection between your body and the ground. Rest your hands on your lap or knees, palms up or down, whatever feels natural. The key is to find a posture that promotes alertness without strain. Picture yourself like a sturdy tree, deeply rooted yet flexible in the breeze.

Breath as Your Anchor: The Gateway to Stillness

AS YOU SETTLE INTO your chosen posture, let's explore the gateway to stillness, the breath. Your breath is not just the rhythm of life; it's the anchor that grounds you in the present moment. Close your eyes gently, take a deep breath in, and exhale slowly. Feel the air fill your lungs and then release, carrying away any tension.

Meditation, at its core, is about mindfulness, being fully present in the moment. The breath becomes your guide, a constant in the ebb and flow of thoughts. As you breathe in, you're here; as you breathe out, you release. The breath is your anchor amidst the sea of thoughts.

Exploring Breath Awareness: A Mindful Pause

LET'S DELVE A BIT DEEPER into breath awareness, a fundamental aspect of many meditation practices. Bring your attention to the sensation of the breath. Feel the coolness as you inhale the warmth as you exhale. Notice the rise and fall of your chest or the gentle expansion of your abdomen.

As you focus on your breath, you might notice the mind's tendency to wander. Thoughts dart like playful butterflies. That's okay; it's the nature of the mind. Gently guide your attention back to the breath. Picture it as a gentle redirection, like steering a boat back on course.

The Dance of Thoughts: Embracing Stillness Amidst the Storm

IN THE DANCE OF MEDITATION, thoughts are the partners—sometimes swirling around, sometimes taking center stage. The misconception is that meditation is about banishing thoughts altogether. Quite the opposite; it's about observing the thoughts without getting entangled in them.

Imagine your thoughts as clouds drifting across the sky. You are the silent observer, watching the clouds come and go. Some are wispy and fleeting; others might linger. But the sky—the vast expanse of your consciousness, remains unchanged. In this stillness, you find a tranquil space amid the storm of thoughts.

The Gentle Art of Guided Meditation: A Voice Amidst Silence

NOW, LET'S INTRODUCE the concept of guided meditation. If sitting in silence feels daunting, guided meditation can be your companion on this journey. It's like having a friendly voice leading you through the landscape of your mind.

Find a guided meditation that resonates with you, it could be a recording, an app, or even a script you read aloud to yourself. Allow the words to guide you, painting pictures in your mind and inviting you into a state of deep relaxation. Guided meditation is a bridge between the external and internal, a pathway to stillness paved with words.

Creating Your Own Script: A Personal Symphony of Relaxation

FOR THE ADVENTUROUS souls, there's the option of creating your own guided meditation script. Picture it as composing a symphony of relaxation tailored to your preferences. Begin with a grounding introduction, invite relaxation with soothing imagery, and guide yourself through a mental journey of tranquility.

Your script can be as simple or elaborate as you desire. Describe a serene beach, a peaceful forest, or a cozy fireside. Your words become the brushstrokes painting a mental canvas. Remember, there's no right or wrong; it's about what feels authentic to you.

Reflecting on Your Journey: The Closing Act

AS YOU CONCLUDE YOUR meditation session, take a moment for reflection. Consider the sensations you experienced, the thoughts that visited, and the stillness you touched. This closing act is not just a ritual; it's an acknowledgment of the time you've dedicated to yourself, a moment of gratitude for the stillness amidst the chaos.

Getting started with meditation is not a grand proclamation but a series of small, deliberate steps. Picture it as a dance, you, in rhythm with your breath, swaying with the currents of thoughts, and finding stillness in the gentle pauses. In the chapters that unfold, we'll explore diverse meditation techniques, but for now, take a deep breath, pat yourself on the back, and savor the stillness you've discovered within. The journey has just begun.

Chapter 4: Different Meditation Techniques

Welcome to the vibrant kaleidoscope of meditation techniques, a world where the art of stillness unfolds in diverse forms. In this chapter, we embark on a journey through the rich tapestry of meditation practices, each weaving a unique thread into the fabric of your inner exploration. So, fasten your seatbelt as we traverse the landscapes of mindfulness, loving-kindness, mantra, and more.

Mindfulness Meditation: Embracing the Present Moment

LET'S BEGIN WITH THE cornerstone of many meditation practices—mindfulness meditation. Picture a serene lake, its surface unruffled by the winds of past regrets or future worries. Mindfulness is the art of being fully present, akin to dipping your toes into the calm waters of the now.

Start by sitting comfortably, anchor your attention on the breath, and let the symphony of the present unfold. Notice the sensations, sounds, and thoughts without judgment. It's not about emptying the mind but observing it like a curious spectator. Mindfulness is the practice of acknowledging each moment, no matter how fleeting.

Loving-Kindness Meditation: Cultivating Compassion

NOW, LET'S DIVE INTO the heart-expanding realm of loving-kindness meditation. Envision a warm, radiant light emanating from your heart, embracing you and extending to others. This practice is about cultivating compassion, starting with you and radiating outward like ripples in a pond.

Begin with a simple phrase like "May I be happy, may I be healthy." As you breathe, extend these wishes to others, loved ones, acquaintances, even those you may find challenging. Loving-kindness is not just a meditation technique; it's a transformative journey that softens the edges of your heart.

Mantra Meditation: The Power of Repetition

ENTER THE RHYTHMIC world of mantra meditation, where words become a gentle current guiding you into tranquility. Imagine a sacred word or phrase repeated like a mantra, a melodious chant echoing through the corridors of your mind.

Your mantra could be a single word, like "peace" or "love," or a Sanskrit phrase with profound meaning. As you repeat it, the vibrations resonate within, quieting the mental chatter. Mantra meditation is not about the meaning of the words but the resonance they create, like a harmonic chord resonating in your soul.

Body Scan Meditation: The Art of Inner Exploration

LET'S SHIFT OUR FOCUS to body scan meditation, a practice that invites you to explore the landscape of your own body. Imagine a gentle spotlight moving through each part, illuminating sensations and inviting relaxation. It's like a gentle massage for your mind.

Lie down or sit comfortably, close your eyes, and bring attention to each part of your body, starting from your toes to the crown of your head. Notice any tension or sensations without the need to change them. Body scan meditation is a journey within, fostering a deep connection between mind and body.

Breathing Meditation: The Lifeline to Stillness

RETURN TO THE SIMPLICITY of breath with breathing meditation. Imagine each breath as a lifeline, a bridge between the outer world and your inner sanctuary. It's not just about the act of breathing; it's about the awareness, the subtle dance between inhales and exhales.

Sit comfortably, close your eyes, and focus on the breath. Notice its rhythm, the rise and fall of your chest or the gentle expansion of your abdomen. In this dance of breath, you discover a lifeline to stillness, a grounding force amidst the whirlwind of thoughts.

Guided Meditation: A Voice Amidst Silence

FOR THOSE WHO SEEK companionship in their meditation journey, guided meditation is your friendly ally. Picture it as a soothing voice leading you through the landscapes of your own mind, a guiding star in the vastness of stillness.

Find a guided meditation that resonates with you, there are countless recordings, apps, or scripts available. Whether it's a virtual walk through a peaceful forest or a journey to your inner sanctuary, guided meditation adds a layer of familiarity to the silent expanses of meditation.

Creating Your Own Meditation: A Personal Symphony

NOW, LET'S DELVE INTO the art of creating your own meditation. Picture it as composing a personal symphony, where each note is a breath, each phrase visualization. Tailor it to your preferences, include elements that resonate with you, whether it's a mental stroll on a beach or a cosmic journey among the stars.

Consider the pace, the tone, and the imagery that feels authentic to you. Your meditation is not a fixed script but an ever-evolving composition, a reflection of your unique journey into stillness.

Movement Meditation: The Dance of Presence

LET'S STEP AWAY FROM the conventional image of a meditator sitting in stillness. Movement meditation invites you to explore the dance of presence through gentle, intentional movements. Imagine swaying like a tree in the breeze or flowing through a sequence of mindful yoga poses.

The essence is not in the complexity of the movements but in the awareness you bring to each action. Movement meditation is a celebration of the body's grace, a dance that harmonizes with the rhythm of your breath and the beat of your heart.

Reflection Meditation: Contemplating Life's Tapestry

AS WE CONCLUDE OUR exploration, let's touch on reflection meditation, a practice of contemplating the threads of your life's tapestry. Picture it as flipping through the pages of a mental photo album, observing the moments, the challenges, and the joys with a gentle curiosity.

Sit in a comfortable position, close your eyes, and let your mind wander through the landscape of memories. Reflection meditation is not about dwelling on the past but acknowledging it with gratitude and learning. It's a conversation with yourself, a moment to honor the journey that has brought you to this present stillness.

In this chapter, we've strolled through a garden of meditation techniques, each offering a unique fragrance to the bouquet of stillness. As you explore these practices, remember there's no one-size-fits-all. Your meditation journey is as unique as your fingerprint, and the technique that resonates with you is the one that paints the colors of serenity in your world. So, take a deep breath, choose a path that beckons, and let the exploration of stillness continue. The journey has just begun.

Chapter 5: The Art of Mindful Living: Finding Harmony in the Present Moment

In the symphony of self-discovery, Chapter 5 unfolds as a melodious exploration into the art of mindful living, a practice that unveils the richness of the present moment, inviting you to dance with the cadence of life's unfolding rhythm.

Awakening the Senses: A Prelude to Mindful Living

AS YOU STEP INTO THE realm of mindful living, let the awakening of the senses be a prelude, a gentle reminder to engage fully with the sensory symphony that surrounds you. Awakening the senses is not a rush; it's a deliberate immersion into the textures, scents, sounds, and hues that paint the canvas of your existence.

Pause and observe the world around you. Feel the warmth of sunlight on your skin, savor the aroma of freshly brewed coffee, listen to the rustle of leaves in the breeze, and notice the vibrant colors that adorn your surroundings. Awakening the senses is not a mere observation; it's an invitation to be present with every nuance of the present moment.

The Dance of Breath: A Ballet of Presence

IN THE BALLET OF MINDFUL living, the dance of breath takes center stage, a rhythmic ballet that anchors you to the present. The dance of breath is not a mechanical routine; it's a graceful flow that connects you to the life force within.

Take a moment to focus on your breath. Inhale deeply, feeling the air fill your lungs, and exhale slowly, releasing any tension. The dance of breath is not a performance; it's a simple, yet profound, act that brings you into the immediacy of the now.

Cultivating Presence in Daily Activities: The Waltz of Conscious Action

AS YOU WALTZ THROUGH the movements of daily life, cultivating presence becomes a graceful dance, a conscious waltz that infuses even routine actions with mindfulness. Cultivating presence is not a disruption of your routine; it's an elevation of ordinary moments into extraordinary experiences.

Whether you're washing dishes, walking, or eating a meal, bring your full attention to the activity at hand. Feel the water on your hands, notice the sensations in your body as you walk, savor the flavors of each bite. Cultivating presence is not a separate practice; it's an integration of mindfulness into the fabric of your daily activities.

The Stillness Within: A Symphony of Inner Quietude

IN THE SYMPHONY OF mindful living, the stillness within resonates as a profound movement, a symphony of inner quietude that unveils a sanctuary amidst the noise of thoughts and external demands. The stillness within is not a distant retreat; it's a sacred space accessible in the midst of life's bustling tempo.

Find a quiet place, close your eyes, and turn your attention inward. Let go of the chatter in your mind and embrace the stillness. The stillness within is not an escape; it's a homecoming to the tranquility that resides at the core of your being.

Mindful Movement: A Tango with Body and Soul

AS YOU ENGAGE IN THE tango of mindful living, mindful movement becomes a dance, a tango that harmonizes your body and soul. Mindful movement is not an exercise routine; it's a celebration of the intricate relationship between your physical and inner self.

Whether it's yoga, tai chi, or a simple stroll, move with awareness. Feel the sensations in your muscles, notice your breath, and be fully present in the act of moving. Mindful movement is not a performance; it's a holistic expression of unity between body and spirit.

The Art of Gratitude: A Canvas of Thankfulness

IN THE CANVAS OF MINDFUL living, the art of gratitude unfolds as a masterpiece, a painting of thankfulness that transforms your perspective on life. The art of gratitude is not a Pollyanna mindset; it's a conscious choice to recognize and appreciate the blessings, both big and small.

Take time each day to reflect on what you're grateful for. It could be the support of loved ones, a moment of serenity, or the simple pleasures that bring joy. The art of gratitude is not wishful thinking; it's a transformative practice that enhances your connection to the abundance woven into your life.

Digital Mindfulness: Balancing Connectivity and Presence

IN THE DIGITAL LANDSCAPE of mindful living, digital mindfulness emerges as a balancing act, a conscious effort to navigate the virtual realm while staying anchored in the present. Digital mindfulness is not a rejection of technology; it's a strategic approach to use it as a tool for connection rather than distraction.

Set boundaries for screen time, practice mindful consumption of digital content, and be intentional about when and how you engage with technology. Digital mindfulness is not a digital detox; it's a harmonious integration that allows you to stay connected without losing touch with the world around you.

Mindful Eating: Savoring the Banquet of Flavors

IN THE BANQUET OF MINDFUL living, mindful eating is a feast, a gastronomic experience that invites you to savor the flavors, textures, and nourishment of each bite. Mindful eating is not a race to finish; it's a deliberate engagement of your senses in the act of nourishing your body.

When you eat, do so with full attention. Notice the colors of your food, appreciate the aromas, and chew slowly to savor the tastes. Mindful eating is not a dietary regime; it's a celebration of the sensory delight inherent in the act of nourishment.

Evening Reflection: A Serenade to the Day's Melody

AS THE DAY'S MELODY reaches its conclusion, the evening reflection unfolds as a serenade, a gentle acknowledgment of the highs and lows, the joys and challenges encountered throughout the day. Evening reflection is not a critical analysis; it's a compassionate review that invites you to integrate the day's experiences.

Take a few moments before bedtime to reflect on the events of the day. Express gratitude for positive moments, acknowledge challenges, and let go of what no longer serves you. Evening reflection is not a guilt trip; it's a tender embrace that prepares you for a restful night.

The Mindful Sleep: A Lullaby for the Soul

IN THE LULLABY OF MINDFUL living, the mindful sleep emerges as a tranquil melody, a lullaby for the soul that nurtures restful and rejuvenating sleep. Mindful sleep is not a mere countdown to the next day; it's a conscious transition that prepares you for a night of deep rest.

Create a calming bedtime routine, disconnect from digital devices, and cultivate an environment conducive to sleep. Mindful sleep is not a remedy for all woes; it's a foundational practice that contributes to your overall well-being.

In the artful dance of mindful living, may you find the grace to fully embrace the present moment, savoring each note of the symphony that is your life. As you waltz through the intricacies of mindful living, may the dance lead you to a deeper connection with yourself and the world around you, creating a harmonious masterpiece of presence and fulfillment.

Chapter 6: The Journey Inward: Advanced Meditation Practices

Welcome to the heart of the meditation labyrinth. In this chapter, we'll plunge into the depths of advanced meditation practices, a realm where the ordinary transforms into the extraordinary. As you embark on this journey inward, be prepared for a tapestry of experiences, from the ethereal realms of transcendental meditation to the ancient wisdom of Vipassana. Let the exploration begin.

Transcendental Meditation: Beyond the Horizon

IMAGINE SAILING INTO the vast expanse of the mind, beyond the horizon of conscious thought. That's the essence of Transcendental Meditation (TM). Developed by Maharishi Mahesh Yogi, TM involves the repetition of a specific mantra. But it's not just any mantra, it's a unique sound that acts as a vessel, carrying you beyond the chattering mind.

To practice TM, find a quiet space, sit comfortably, close your eyes, and silently repeat your mantra. As you dive deeper into the repetition, thoughts begin to fade, and you touch the stillness within. TM is like surfing the waves of consciousness, riding into the expanses where words and thoughts dissolve.

Zen Meditation: The Art of Silent Illumination

ZEN, THE WORD ITSELF conjures images of ancient monasteries, cherry blossoms, and the silent illumination of the mind. Zen meditation, or Zazen, is simplicity at its finest. Picture sitting in stillness, focusing on your breath, and letting go of the mental clutter.

To practice Zazen, find a quiet space, sit on a cushion or chair, and assume a stable posture. Breathe naturally, paying attention to each inhalation and exhalation. The beauty of Zen lies in the simplicity of just sitting. Thoughts come and go like clouds in the sky, but you remain the silent witness.

Vipassana Meditation: Insight into the Self

VIPASSANA, MEANING "clear seeing" or "insight," is a potent meditation technique with roots tracing back to ancient India. Developed by Gautama Buddha, Vipassana is not just a practice; it's a profound journey into self-discovery. Picture it as a mental surgery where you dissect layers of your own consciousness.

In a Vipassana retreat, practitioners observe noble silence, abstain from any form of communication, and delve into the intricacies of their own minds. The focus is on observing bodily sensations with unwavering attention, recognizing the impermanence of sensations, and understanding the deep interconnection of mind and matter. Vipassana is not for the faint of heart, but for those who seek profound insight into the nature of reality.

Chakra Meditation: Aligning Energy Centers

ENTER THE REALM OF Chakra Meditation, a practice rooted in the ancient yogic traditions of India. Picture the body as an intricate network of energy centers, each associated with different aspects of your being. Chakra meditation is the art of aligning and balancing these energy hubs.

To practice Chakra Meditation, find a comfortable position, close your eyes, and bring awareness to each chakra, starting from the base of the spine (Muladhara) to the crown of the head (Sahasrara). Visualize each chakra as a spinning wheel of light, and as you focus on them, you bring harmony to the subtle energies within. Chakra meditation is a journey into the vibrant symphony of your own energy.

Loving-Kindness Meditation (Metta): Cultivating Boundless Love

WE'VE TOUCHED ON LOVING-Kindness Meditation before, but in its advanced form, known as Metta; it becomes a powerful force for cultivating boundless love. Picture the expansion of your heart, radiating love and goodwill not just to yourself and loved ones but to all sentient beings.

In Metta Meditation, find a comfortable seat, close your eyes, and start by directing loving-kindness towards yourself. Then, expand it gradually to include friends, acquaintances, those you may have conflicts with, and eventually, to all living beings. Metta is like sending out ripples of love, creating a harmonious resonance in the universe.

Mindfulness-Based Stress Reduction (MBSR): Integrating Mindfulness into Life

MINDFULNESS-BASED STRESS Reduction (MBSR), developed by Dr. Jon Kabat-Zinn, is not just a meditation technique; it's a way of life. MBSR integrates mindfulness into daily activities, fostering a deep sense of presence and resilience in the face of stress.

In MBSR, practitioners engage in various mindfulness practices, including body scan meditations, mindful breathing, and awareness of daily activities. The goal is not just to find stillness on the cushion but to carry the essence of mindfulness into the flow of life. MBSR is a bridge between the tranquility of meditation and the vibrancy of everyday existence.

Yoga Nidra: The Yogic Sleep

YOGA NIDRA, OFTEN REFERRED to as "yogic sleep," is a state of conscious relaxation that transcends the borders of wakefulness and sleep. Picture it as a journey where you lie down, close your eyes, and follow the guidance of a teacher through various stages of relaxation.

Yoga Nidra takes you to the threshold of sleep while maintaining awareness. As you journey through body awareness, breath, and visualization, you enter a state of deep relaxation. It's not about doing; it's about being. Yoga Nidra is a rejuvenating voyage into the sanctuary of your own consciousness.

Kundalini Meditation: Awakening the Serpent Power

KUNDALINI, THE DORMANT energy coiled at the base of the spine, likened to a serpent waiting to be awakened. Kundalini Meditation is a practice that aims to arouse this latent energy and channel it through the energy centers of the body.

In Kundalini Meditation, practitioners engage in dynamic movements, breath work, and chanting to awaken and raise the Kundalini energy. Picture it as an inner journey where the serpent of energy ascends through the spine, unlocking higher states of consciousness. Kundalini Meditation is not just a physical practice; it's a mystical expedition into the realms of the sublime.

Silent Retreats: Immersion in Stillness

SILENT RETREATS, THE monastic sanctuaries where words are sparse, and the silence is pregnant with wisdom. Whether it's a Vipassana retreat or a silent meditation immersion, these retreats offer a profound experience of stillness.

Picture days where communication is limited to essential gestures, where the mind has space to unfurl its wings without the constraints of words. Silent retreats are not just a break from the noise of the world; they are an immersion in the symphony of inner quietude, a pilgrimage to the sacred spaces within.

In the realms of advanced meditation, the ordinary transforms into the extraordinary, and the mind becomes a canvas for painting the hues of transcendence. As you explore these practices, remember it's not about achieving a specific state; it's about the journey, the unfolding mystery of your own consciousness. So, take a deep breath, step into the realms of advanced meditation, and let the inner odyssey continue. The journey has just begun.

Chapter 7: Mindful Living: Integrating Meditation into Daily Life

Welcome to the art of mindful living, an exquisite dance between the tranquility of meditation and the vibrant tapestry of everyday existence. In this chapter, we'll explore how to seamlessly weave the wisdom of meditation into the fabric of your daily life. It's not just about finding serenity on the cushion; it's about carrying that serenity into the bustling symphony of your world. So, let's dive into the practical magic of mindful living.

Morning Rituals: The Symphony of Dawn

PICTURE THE DAWN, A canvas painted with hues of soft pinks and gentle golds. Your morning rituals are the brushes that shape the masterpiece of your day. Instead of diving headfirst into the chaos, start with a mindful moment. As you wake, take a few deep breaths, feel the warmth of the sunlight, and set an intention for the day.

Create a sacred space for your morning rituals. It could be a cozy corner with a cushion or a chair. As you sip your coffee or tea, let each sip be a reminder to savor the moment. Morning rituals are not just routines; they're the overture to a mindful day.

Mindful Eating: Savoring the Symphony of Flavors

EATING IS NOT JUST a biological necessity; it's a sensory symphony. Mindful eating is the art of savoring each note, each flavor, without rushing through the movements. Picture a table set with colors, textures, and aromas, a feast for the senses.

Before you start, take a moment of gratitude for the food on your plate. As you eat, engage your senses. Notice the textures, taste each bite, and savor the flavors. Put down your fork between bites. Mindful eating is not about restriction; it's about reveling in the banquet of sensations.

Workplace Mindfulness: Finding Stillness Amidst the Hustle

THE WORKPLACE, A BUSTLING arena of tasks, deadlines, and the occasional office drama. But amidst the chaos, you can find stillness. Mindfulness at work is not about escaping; it's about navigating the currents with grace.

In the midst of emails and meetings, take short mindfulness breaks. Close your eyes, take a few deep breaths, and reset. Use the act of typing as a grounding exercise. Feel the keys beneath your fingertips, the rhythmic dance of your fingers. Workplace mindfulness is not a grand gesture; it's a series of small, intentional pauses in the symphony of the workday.

Mindful Movement: Dancing with Presence

EXERCISE IS NOT JUST a physical endeavor; it's a dance with the present moment. Whether it's a brisk walk, yoga, or a gym session, infuse mindfulness into your movement. Picture it as a conversation between your body and the present moment.

As you move, pay attention to the sensations. Feel the ground beneath your feet, the stretch in your muscles, and the rhythm of your breath. Exercise is not just a means to an end; it's a celebration of what your body can do in this moment. Mindful movement is not about reaching a finish line; it's about savoring each step of the journey.

Digital Mindfulness: Navigating the Information Ocean

THE DIGITAL LANDSCAPE, an ocean of information, notifications, and the occasional social media whirlpool. Instead of getting swept away, navigate with mindfulness. Picture your digital devices not as distractions but as tools for intentional living.

Set boundaries for your digital space. During meals or moments of rest, silence the notifications. When you check emails or scroll through social media, do it with intention. Notice how the digital world affects your thoughts and emotions. Digital mindfulness is not about disconnection; it's about conscious engagement.

Mindful Relationships: Cultivating Connection

IN THE INTRICATE DANCE of relationships, mindfulness is the gentle partner that leads. Whether with family, friends, or colleagues, picture each interaction as a dance of presence. Instead of waiting for your turn to speak, and thinking about what you are going to say, listen with your whole being.

During conversations, be fully present. Notice the nuances in the other person's words, the cadence of their voice. It will tell you more about the person's frame of mind than the words they speak. Put away the distractions; let your phone rest. Mindful relationships are not about grand gestures; they're about the subtle, everyday dances that cultivate connection.

Evening Reflections: The Symphony of Gratitude

AS THE DAY CONCLUDES, embrace the evening reflections, a moment to savor the symphony of experiences. Picture it as a gratitude ritual, a pause to acknowledge the melodies and harmonies of the day.

Before bedtime, take a few moments for reflection. What moments brought you joy? What challenges did you navigate with resilience? Express gratitude for the simple joys and the lessons learned. Evening reflections are not about judgment; they're about embracing the fullness of your day with a grateful heart.

Mindful Sleep: Surrendering to Stillness

AS YOU TRANSITION INTO the realm of dreams, let sleep be a mindful surrender. Picture it as a gentle descent into stillness, a voyage into the sanctuary of your own consciousness.

Create a bedtime ritual that signals your mind it's time to unwind. It could be reading a book, gentle stretching, or a few moments of deep breathing. As you lie down, feel the touch of the sheets, the gentle darkness enveloping you. Mindful sleep is not about control; it's about surrendering to the natural rhythm of rest.

Weekend Retreats: Escaping to Stillness

IN THE SYMPHONY OF life, weekends are like a tranquil interlude. Use them as mini-retreats, moments to escape the cacophony and dive into stillness. Whether it's a nature walk, a reading retreat, or simply lounging in your favorite spot, make it a mindful affair.

Weekend retreats are not about extravagant plans; they're about carving intentional pockets of stillness. Picture yourself as the conductor of this mini-retreat, orchestrating moments of solitude, joy, and connection. The weekend is not just a break; it's a composition of mindful pauses.

In the rhythm of mindful living, each moment is a note, and you are the composer. It's not about creating a grand opus but about crafting a symphony of presence in the ordinary moments. So, take a deep breath, let the music of mindful living guide you, and dance through the tapestry of your days. The journey continues, harmonizing the stillness within with the melody of life.

Chapter 8: Embracing Challenges on the Meditation Path

Ah, the meditation path, a journey filled with serenity, self-discovery, and, yes, challenges. In this chapter, we'll don our adventurer's hat and explore the rugged terrains of obstacles that might crop up on your meditation sojourn. But fear not, for each challenge is a stepping stone, a hidden doorway to deeper understanding and resilience. So, let's lace up those boots and trek through the landscapes of difficulties on the path to inner stillness.

The Myth of Perfect Meditation: Embracing Imperfection

FIRSTLY, LET'S DEBUNK the myth of perfect meditation. It doesn't exist. If you're expecting a Hollywood-style montage of serene moments and zero distractions, it's time to let that notion float away like a passing cloud. Meditation is not about achieving perfection; it's about embracing the imperfections of the present moment.

Your mind will wander, that's what minds do. Thoughts will interrupt your serenity, that's part of the process. Instead of striving for an elusive perfection, consider each meditation session a unique journey. Embrace the imperfections with a gentle smile, for in the dance between focus and distraction, you discover the true essence of meditation.

The Restless Mind: Taming the Wild Horses

AH, THE RESTLESS MIND, a wild herd of thoughts galloping through the vast landscapes of your consciousness. It's normal, and it happens to everyone. Picture it as trying to corral wild horses; they'll resist a bit before settling.

When your mind resembles a bustling marketplace, gently guide it back to the present moment. Use your breath as the reins. Inhale, exhale, and notice the thoughts without judgment. The restless mind is not an adversary; it's a spirited companion on your meditation journey. As you tame the wild horses of your thoughts, you'll find a deeper connection with the stillness within.

The Time Conundrum: Navigating Busy Schedules

IN THE HUSTLE AND BUSTLE of daily life, finding time for meditation can feel like locating a needle in a haystack. But here's the truth, you don't need an hour-long session atop a mountain. Even a few minutes count. Picture meditation as a mini-vacation for your mind amidst the busyness.

Instead of waiting for the perfect time, seize the moments within your schedule. Whether it's during a lunch break, waiting for a meeting, or before bedtime, those pockets of time are gold mines for mindfulness. The time conundrum is not a barrier; it's an invitation to infuse stillness into the rhythm of your day.

Physical Discomfort: The Body's Protest

SITTING CROSS-LEGGED like a serene Buddha may seem picturesque, but the reality is your body might rebel. Aching knees, a sore back, physical discomfort is the body's way of protesting the rigid posture.

Here's the magic word: adapt. You don't have to mimic statues; find a position that suits you. Whether it's sitting on a chair, using cushions, or lying down, make meditation a comfortable experience. Physical discomfort is not a punishment; it's a signal to listen to your body and find a posture that aligns with your unique comfort.

The Expectation Trap: Liberating Your Mind

EXPECTATIONS ARE THE silent architects of disappointment. If you enter each meditation session with a checklist of what it should be, you might find yourself tangled in the expectation trap. Meditation is not a performance; it's an exploration.

Let go of preconceived notions. Instead of expecting a particular experience, approach each session with curiosity. Whether it's calm or chaotic, each meditation is a step on the path. The expectation trap is not a maze; it's an open field where you liberate your mind from the shackles of predetermined outcomes.

The Comparison Game: Your Unique Journey

IN THE REALM OF MEDITATION, there's no room for the comparison game. "Karen meditates for an hour daily, and I struggle with ten minutes." Each journey is unique. Comparisons are like mirages, they distort reality.

Your meditation practice is as individual as your fingerprint. Instead of measuring against others, measure against yourself. Celebrate your progress, no matter how incremental. The comparison game is not a race; it's a distraction from the rich landscape of your own meditation journey.

Impatience and Frustration: Weathering the Storm

IMPATIENCE AND FRUSTRATION, the storms that may cloud your meditation sky. "Why am I not getting this right?" Impatience is a gentle reminder that you're human, not a meditation robot.

When frustration knocks, invite it in for tea. It's not an adversary; it's a passing cloud. Weather the storm with patience. Impatience and frustration are not hurdles; they're the winds that sculpt the landscape of your resilience.

Inconsistency: Embracing the Ebb and Flow

INCONSISTENCY IS NOT a meditation sin; it's a reality. Life's currents are unpredictable. Instead of beating yourself up for missing a day or a week, acknowledge the ebb and flow of your meditation journey.

Meditation is forgiving. It's not about rigid routines but the flexibility to flow with the currents of life. Inconsistency is not a failure; it's an opportunity to return, to rediscover the stillness amidst the waves of life.

The Monkey Mind: Dancing with Distractions

THE MONKEY MIND, EVER so playful, leaping from branch to branch of thoughts. Distractions are not enemies; they're the companions on your meditation safari.

Instead of trying to cage the monkey mind, dance with it. Acknowledge the thoughts, let them pass, and gently guide your focus back to the present moment. The monkey mind is not a hindrance; it's a reminder that your mind is alive and kicking.

Feeling Stuck: A Pause, Not a Dead End

FEELING STUCK IN YOUR meditation is not a dead end; it's a pause, a moment to reassess. The stillness might seem elusive, but it's not a destination. It's a journey.

If you find yourself circling the same mental pathways, switch directions. Try a different meditation technique, explore guided sessions, or take a break. Feeling stuck is not a roadblock; it's an invitation to chart a new course.

In the grand tapestry of meditation, challenges are not adversaries; they're the colors that add depth and richness to the journey. Embrace them, dance with them, and let each challenge be a guide, a teacher on your path to inner stillness. The adventure continues, and with each step, you discover the resilience and wisdom within.

Chapter 9: The Art of Mindful Breathing

Ah, the breath, the gentle rhythm that intertwines with the dance of life. In this chapter, we'll embark on a journey into the heart of mindfulness through the art of mindful breathing. Imagine the breath as your steadfast companion, guiding you through the tapestry of each moment. It's not just inhaling and exhaling; it's a doorway to profound presence, a sanctuary in the midst of life's bustling symphony.

The Symphony of Breath: An Overture to Mindfulness

CLOSE YOUR EYES AND take a deep breath. Feel the air entering your lungs, expanding your chest, and then gently releasing. That's the symphony of breath, an overture to mindfulness. In each inhalation and exhalation, there's a world of sensations waiting to be explored.

Mindful breathing is not about controlling the breath but about witnessing its natural cadence. Picture it as attending a concert of sensations, the cool touch as you inhale, the warmth as you exhale. The symphony of breath is a perpetual performance, and you have a front-row seat.

The Present Moment Gateway: Breath as Your Guide

IN THE GRAND THEATER of your mind, the breath is the guide to the present moment. When the curtains of past regrets or future anxieties draw, the breath remains, a constant anchor. Picture it as the gateway to a timeless realm, the now.

To practice, find a comfortable seat, close your eyes, and turn your attention to the breath. Notice the rise and fall of your chest or the sensation of air passing through your nostrils. As thoughts meander like actors on a stage, let the breath be the director, bringing you back to the present moment. The gateway to the present moment is not hidden; it's right beneath your nose.

The Dance of Inhalation and Exhalation: A Choreography of Calm

INHALE, EXHALE, A DANCE as old as life itself. The breath, like a dance partner, engages in choreography of calm. Each inhalation infuses vitality; each exhalation releases tension. It's a duet between the body and the breath, a dance of renewal.

As you breathe, let your awareness follow the inhalation and exhalation. Picture it as a graceful dance, inhale, a rising movement of energy; exhale, a gentle release. The dance of inhalation and exhalation is not a performance; it's a rhythm that harmonizes with the melody of your being.

Body as the Canvas: Sensations in the Breath Brushstrokes

THE BODY, AN EXQUISITE canvas waiting to be painted by the brushstrokes of breath. As you breathe, sensations unfold, creating a masterpiece of awareness. Picture the breath as the brush, gently caressing the canvas of your body.

Scan your body with each breath. Feel the expansion in your chest, the subtle rise in your abdomen. Notice the sensations in your nostrils as the air flows in and out. The body as the canvas is not static; it's a living, breathing artwork, and the breath is the artist's touch.

Counting Breath: A Musical Score for Focus

IN THE SYMPHONY OF mindful breathing, counting breath is a musical score for focus. When the mind's orchestra gets too loud, counting becomes the gentle conductor, bringing harmony to the cacophony of thoughts. Picture it as marking each breath with a note, creating a melody of concentration.

To practice, inhale and silently count "one," then exhale. Inhale, count "two," and then exhale. Continue until you reach ten and start again. If your mind wanders, acknowledge it, and return to one. Counting breath is not a rigid structure; it's a flexible score that guides your attention back to the breath's melody.

Box Breathing: Creating a Breath Sanctuary

IN THE HUSTLE OF LIFE, creating a breath sanctuary is a gift to your mind and body. Box breathing, also known as square breathing, is a technique that transforms each breath into a harmonious sanctuary. Picture it as building the walls of serenity around your breath.

Inhale for a count of four, hold the breath for four, exhale for four, and then pause for four. Repeat this rhythmic pattern. Box breathing is not a confined space; it's a sanctuary you carry within, a refuge where each breath becomes a moment of peace.

Deep Belly Breathing: Riding the Waves of Relaxation

WHEN STRESS SURGES like turbulent waves, deep belly breathing is your surfboard. This technique taps into the diaphragm, inviting relaxation to ride the waves of each breath. Picture it as a journey into the depths of calm.

Place one hand on your chest and the other on your abdomen. Inhale deeply, allowing your abdomen to expand. Feel the breath fill your lower lungs, then exhale fully. Deep belly breathing is not a struggle against the waves; it's riding them with the grace of relaxation.

Sensory Breathing: A Symphony of Senses

THE BREATH IS NOT CONFINED to the nose; it's a symphony that resonates through all your senses. Sensory breathing invites you to explore the touch, taste, and smell of each breath, creating a multisensory experience. Picture it as an orchestra of sensations.

As you inhale, notice the coolness of the air entering your nostrils. Taste the freshness on your tongue. Feel the expansion in your chest and the subtle vibrations in your body. Sensory breathing is not limited to the nose; it's an exploration of the breath's rich texture through all your senses.

Guided Visualization: Breath as Your Inner Guide

IN THE REALM OF MINDFUL breathing, the breath becomes your inner guide in guided visualizations. Picture it as a journey where each breath propels you through vivid landscapes of your mind. Whether it's a serene beach or a lush forest, let the breath guide you.

Close your eyes and breathe naturally. As you inhale, visualize yourself walking along a peaceful path. Feel the textures, hear the sounds, and let the breath be the guide through this inner landscape. Guided visualization is not an escape; it's a conscious journey where the breath is both the compass and the companion.

In the art of mindful breathing, each inhalation and exhalation is a brushstroke, painting the canvas of your awareness. Whether it's the dance of inhalation and exhalation or the symphony of sensations, the breath is your ever-present companion in the journey of mindfulness. So, take a deep breath, let the symphony begin, and allow the breath to guide you through the landscapes of each precious moment.

Chapter 10: The Power of Mindful Visualization

Welcome to the enchanting realm of mindful visualization, a practice that transcends the boundaries of the ordinary and opens the door to the extraordinary. In this chapter, we'll embark on a journey into the art of seeing with the mind's eye, where imagination becomes a tool for transformation. Picture it as a magical tapestry woven with the threads of your thoughts and emotions, creating a vibrant mosaic of possibilities.

Imagination Unleashed: The Canvas of Mindful Visualization

IMAGINATION IS NOT just for children; it's a boundless canvas waiting for the strokes of your thoughts. Mindful visualization is the act of painting with the colors of your mind. Imagine your mind as an artist's palette, ready to create landscapes of serenity, scenes of success, and portraits of peace.

To begin, find a quiet space, close your eyes, and take a few deep breaths. As you exhale, let go of the clutter of thoughts. Now, let your imagination take the lead. Picture a serene beach, a lush forest, or a cozy room. The canvas of mindful visualization is not limited; it's a vast expanse where you are both the artist and the masterpiece.

Creating Your Inner Sanctuary: A Haven of Peace

IN THE HUSTLE OF LIFE, your mind can be a haven of peace. Mindful visualization allows you to create your inner sanctuary, a place where tranquility is not a fleeting visitor but a permanent resident. Picture it as building the walls of a sanctuary within, a refuge where the storms of life can't reach.

Imagine a place that resonates with peace. It could be a mountain retreat, a sun-kissed meadow, or even a hammock in your backyard. With each breath, visualize the details, the colors, the textures, the sounds. Your inner sanctuary is not a figment; it's a construction of peace within the architecture of your mind.

Goal Setting with Visualization: Painting Your Path to Success

GOALS ARE NOT JUST destinations; they're journeys waiting to be painted with the hues of mindful visualization. Whether it's a career milestone, a fitness target, or a personal aspiration, visualizing your goals adds a layer of motivation and clarity. Picture it as sketching the map to your success.

To practice, envision the endpoint of your goal. If it's a career achievement, see yourself in that leadership role. If it's a fitness goal, visualize the vibrant energy in your workouts. Feel the emotions associated with success, the pride, the joy, the fulfillment. Goal setting with visualization is not wishful thinking; it's a strategic brushstroke on the canvas of your aspirations.

Healing through Visualization: Mending the Body and Mind

THE MIND-BODY CONNECTION is a profound tapestry, and mindful visualization is a healing thread woven into its fabric. Whether you're navigating physical discomfort, stress, or illness, visualization can be a gentle balm for the body and mind. Picture it as a process of mending through the power of your thoughts.

To begin, find a comfortable position, close your eyes, and take a few deep breaths. Imagine a healing light surrounding the area of discomfort. With each breath, visualize this light infusing warmth and comfort. If it's stress or anxiety, picture a gentle stream washing away the tension. Healing through visualization is not a substitute for professional care, but it can be a supportive ally in your wellness journey.

Mindful Visualization for Stress Reduction: A Mental Spa

STRESS, A UBIQUITOUS companion in our fast-paced lives. Mindful visualization offers you a mental spa, a space where stress melts away like snow under the warm sun. Picture it as a retreat for your mind, a place where relaxation is the currency.

Sit or lie down in a comfortable position, close your eyes, and take a few deep breaths. Now, visualize a serene scene, a tranquil beach, a meadow of wildflowers, or a peaceful lake. Feel the sensations, the warmth of the sun, the softness of the grass. As you breathe, let each exhale release the grip of stress. Mindful visualization for stress reduction is not an escape; it's a conscious choice to create moments of tranquility in the midst of chaos.

Enhancing Performance through Visualization: The Mind's Dress Rehearsal

WHETHER YOU'RE AN ATHLETE, a performer, or facing a crucial presentation, mindful visualization is your mind's dress rehearsal. Picture it as a way to fine-tune your performance before the actual stage. Visualization enhances the neural pathways, preparing your mind and body for peak performance.

Sit in a quiet space, close your eyes, and visualize yourself excelling in your endeavor. If it's a sports event, see yourself making that winning shot. If it's a presentation, visualize yourself speaking confidently and engagingly. Feel the emotions associated with success. Enhancing performance through visualization is not a guarantee, but it's a potent tool in the toolkit of excellence.

Cultivating Positive Habits: Planting Seeds of Change

HABITS SHAPE OUR LIVES, and mindful visualization is the gardener planting seeds of positive change. Whether you're working on breaking a habit or cultivating a new one, visualization amplifies the power of intention. Picture it as nurturing the soil of your subconscious mind.

Close your eyes and envision yourself engaged in the positive habit. If it's a healthier lifestyle, visualize making nourishing food choices and enjoying invigorating exercise. If it's a habit of mindfulness, see yourself seamlessly integrating moments of stillness into your day. Cultivating positive habits through visualization is not wishful thinking; it's a deliberate act of sowing seeds that can blossom into transformative change.

Mindful Visualization for Creativity: The Muse within

CREATIVITY IS NOT A mystical force reserved for a chosen few; it's a bubbling spring within, waiting to be tapped. Mindful visualization invites your inner muse to dance. Picture it as unlocking the gates to a reservoir of creative potential.

Sit in a quiet space, close your eyes, and take a few deep breaths. Visualize a space of boundless creativity. It could be an artist's studio, a library of ideas, or a cosmic playground. As you breathe, feel the floodgates of creativity opening. Mindful visualization for creativity is not a quest for perfection; it's a joyful exploration of the vast landscapes of your imaginative mind.

Visualization as a Tool for Gratitude: A Tapestry of Thankfulness

GRATITUDE IS NOT JUST a fleeting emotion; it's a practice that can be amplified through mindful visualization. Picture it as weaving a tapestry of thankfulness, where each thread is a moment of appreciation. Visualization becomes a lens through which you see the beauty in the ordinary.

Sit in a comfortable position, close your eyes, and take a few deep breaths. Visualize moments in your life that evoke gratitude. It could be a supportive friend, a beautiful sunset, or a simple act of kindness. Feel the warmth in your heart as you breathe. Visualization as a tool for gratitude is not about grand gestures; it's about recognizing and appreciating the mosaic of blessings in your life.

In the enchanting landscape of mindful visualization, you are both the artist and the beholder. Whether you're painting scenes of serenity, visualizing your goals, or cultivating positive habits, the canvas is yours to explore. So, close your eyes, take a deep breath, and let the brushstrokes of mindful visualization paint a vibrant mural of possibilities in the gallery of your mind. The journey continues, and with each visualization, you create new pathways to the realms of transformation and self-discovery.

Chapter 11: The Mind-Body Connection: Harmonizing the Symphony Within

Welcome to the extraordinary exploration of the mind-body connection, a profound dance where thoughts, emotions, and physical well-being converge. In this chapter, we'll venture into the intricate interplay between your mental landscape and the sensations of your body. Picture it as a symphony where each note of mindfulness and awareness contributes to the harmonious balance between mind and body.

The Symphony of Sensations: Tuning into the Present Moment

CLOSE YOUR EYES AND take a moment to tune into the symphony of sensations within your body. The gentle rise and fall of your chest with each breath, the subtle heartbeat, the warmth in your palms, these are the melodies of your existence. Picture it as attending a concert where your body is both the stage and the audience.

To practice, find a comfortable position, close your eyes, and take a few deep breaths. As you inhale, feel the expansion in your chest; as you exhale, notice the gentle release. Scan your body with awareness, from the crown of your head to the tips of your toes. The symphony of sensations is not a background noise; it's a rich, vibrant composition playing in the present moment.

Breath as the Conductor: Guiding the Symphony

IN THE GRAND ORCHESTRATION of the mind-body connection, the breath assumes the role of a wise conductor, guiding the symphony of sensations. Picture it as the baton that directs the ebb and flow of your internal concert.

As you breathe, imagine the breath conducting a rhythmic dance through your body. With each inhalation, feel the energy surging; with each exhalation, experience a gentle release. The breath as the conductor is not a dictator; it's a guide, orchestrating a harmonious relationship between your mind and body.

Body Scan Meditation: A Journey of Awareness

BODY SCAN MEDITATION is your passport to a profound journey of awareness, where the mind explores the landscapes of the body. Picture it as a mindful expedition, where each breath is a step into the richness of your physical being.

Lie down or sit comfortably, close your eyes, and begin to scan your body from head to toe. As you breathe, bring attention to each part, noticing any sensations without judgment. The body scan is not a diagnostic tool; it's a voyage of self-discovery, a way to foster a deeper connection between your mind and the physical vessel it inhabits.

Emotions as Crescendos: The Language of the Body

EMOTIONS ARE NOT MERE ephemeral experiences; they are the crescendos in the symphony of the mind-body connection. Picture it as a language your body speaks, each emotion resonating in a unique note.

When you feel joy, notice the lightness in your step and the warmth in your chest. When sadness visits, feel the weight in your shoulders and the softness in your breath. Emotions as crescendos are not disruptions; they're integral passages in the composition of your holistic well-being.

Mindful Eating: Savoring the Gastronomic Symphony

EATING IS NOT JUST a physical act; it's a gastronomic symphony where the mind and body engage in a sensory dance. Picture it as a banquet where each bite is a note, and every flavor is a harmonious chord.

During your meals, practice mindful eating. Take a moment to appreciate the colors and textures of your food. As you chew, savor the flavors and notice the sensations. Mindful eating is not a rushed act; it's a celebration of the symphony of tastes and the nourishment it provides to both mind and body.

Physical Posture: The Body's Silent Language

THE WAY YOU CARRY YOURSELF is not just a matter of posture; it's a silent language your body speaks to the world and, more importantly, to your mind. Picture it as a conversation between your physical form and your mental state.

Whether sitting or standing, pay attention to your posture. Feel the alignment of your spine, the grounding of your feet. Notice how a straight posture fosters a sense of alertness, while a relaxed stance communicates ease. Physical posture is not just an external display; it's a communication channel that influences the dialogue between your mind and body.

Mind-Body Breathing: Fusion of Energy

BREATH, THE CONDUCTOR of the mind-body symphony, becomes even more powerful when infused with intention. Mind-body breathing is the fusion of breath and energy, where each inhale revitalizes and each exhale releases. Picture it as a dance of energy circulating through your being.

To practice, find a comfortable position, close your eyes, and take a few deep breaths. As you inhale, visualize energy flowing through your body, nourishing each cell. As you exhale, imagine releasing any tension or negativity. Mind-body breathing is not a separation; it's a conscious integration of the life force that breath brings.

Embodying Gratitude: A Practice of Wholeness

GRATITUDE IS NOT JUST an attitude; it's a practice that resonates in every cell of your body. Picture it as a gentle shower of appreciation, permeating your being and fostering a sense of wholeness.

Sit or stand comfortably, close your eyes, and take a few deep breaths. With each inhale, feel gratitude expanding within you. As you exhale, let this sense of gratitude radiate outward. Embodying gratitude is not a ritual; it's a conscious choice to acknowledge the interconnectedness of your mind and body.

Release and Relaxation: An Overture to Well-Being

IN THE SYMPHONY OF the mind-body connection, release and relaxation compose the overture to well-being. Picture it as a musical pause, where each breath is a release, and each moment of stillness is a note of relaxation.

Lie down, close your eyes, and allow your body to soften into the ground. As you breathe, consciously release any tension. Picture the breath as a gentle breeze, sweeping away stress and leaving a trail of calm. Release and relaxation are not luxuries; they're essential movements in the symphony of holistic well-being.

The mind-body connection is not an abstract concept; it's a lived experience, a dance where each movement of the mind is echoed in the sensations of the body. As you continue this exploration, remember that you are both the composer and the audience in the extraordinary symphony of your own existence. Listen, feel, and let the harmonies of mindfulness and awareness guide you towards a deeper understanding of the intricate connection between your mind and body.

Chapter 12: The Serenity of Sound: A Symphony for the Soul

Step into the ethereal realm of sound, where vibrations create a tapestry of emotions and harmony resonates with the deepest layers of your soul. In this chapter, we'll delve into the power of sound and explore how it can be a transformative force in your journey toward happiness and inner peace. Picture it as a symphony for the soul, where each note carries the promise of serenity and self-discovery.

The Language of Sound: A Universal Dialogue

SOUND IS NOT JUST AN auditory experience; it's a universal language that speaks to the core of human experience. Picture it as a dialogue that transcends words, reaching deep into the recesses of your emotions and thoughts.

Take a moment to listen, truly listen, to the sounds around you. The rustling leaves, the distant hum of traffic, or the rhythmic patter of rain, each sound is a note in the universal symphony. The language of sound is not confined to ears alone; it's an invitation for your entire being to engage in a dialogue with the world.

The Healing Melody: Nurturing the Soul

SOUND HAS THE EXTRAORDINARY ability to heal, like a gentle balm for the soul. Picture it as a melody that caresses the wounded parts of your being, offering solace and rejuvenation.

Explore the healing power of sound by incorporating soothing music into your daily routine. It could be the soft strumming of a guitar, the melodic tunes of a piano, or the calming sounds of nature. Let the healing melody weave through the fabric of your day, creating pockets of tranquility. The healing melody is not a magical cure; it's a tender companion on your journey toward emotional well-being.

Mindful Listening: An Art of Presence

IN THE RUSH OF MODERN life, listening has become a rarity. Mindful listening is an art—an art of presence that allows you to fully immerse yourself in the symphony of sounds. Picture it as a dance where you become one with the music, the laughter, and the whispers of existence.

Choose a moment to practice mindful listening. It could be a conversation with a friend, the rustle of leaves during a walk, or the gentle hum of your surroundings. As you listen, be fully present. Let go of the impulse to respond or analyze. Mindful listening is not a passive act; it's an active participation in the rich tapestry of the present moment.

The Power of Silence: A Pinnacle of Sound

SILENCE, THE CANVAS upon which sound paints its masterpiece. In the symphony of life, silence is not an absence; it's a powerful presence, a moment pregnant with possibilities. Picture it as a canvas awaiting the brushstrokes of sound to create a masterpiece.

Explore the power of silence by intentionally carving out moments of quiet in your day. It could be a few minutes of meditation, a contemplative walk, or simply sitting in stillness. As you embrace silence, notice the subtle sounds that emerge, the distant hum, the rustle of leaves, or the beating of your own heart. The power of silence is not a void; it's a space where the essence of sound finds its purest expression.

Sound Bath Meditation: Immersed in Vibrations

SOUND BATH MEDITATION is a journey of immersion, where the vibrations of sound become a gentle current carrying you to a state of deep relaxation. Picture it as a sensory bath where the frequencies of sound cleanse the palette of your emotions.

Lie down in a comfortable position, close your eyes, and let the sounds wash over you. It could be the resonant tones of singing bowls, the soft strumming of a harp, or the rhythmic beat of a drum. Allow the vibrations to permeate every cell of your being. Sound bath meditation is not an escape; it's a conscious dive into the ocean of sound, where each wave carries you deeper into tranquility.

Chanting and Mantras: Sacred Sound Exploration

CHANTING AND MANTRAS are ancient tools that harness the power of sound for spiritual exploration. Picture it as a sacred journey where the vibrations of your voice become a vehicle for inner transformation.

Experiment with chanting a simple mantra or affirmations. It could be as uncomplicated as chanting "Om" or repeating affirmations like "I am at peace." Feel the resonance in your chest as the sound emanates. Chanting and mantras are not rituals; they're gateways to a sacred space within you.

Creating Your Sound Sanctuary: Personalized Bliss

YOUR ENVIRONMENT PLAYS a crucial role in your emotional well-being, and creating a personalized sound sanctuary is a delightful way to curate your surroundings. Picture it as crafting a haven where each sound contributes to a symphony of bliss.

Identify sounds that bring you joy and calmness. It could be instrumental music, the sounds of nature, or even recorded affirmations. Designate a space in your home where these sounds can envelop you, creating a cocoon of tranquility. Your sound sanctuary is not a luxury; it's a conscious choice to infuse your surroundings with positive vibrations.

Dance to Your Own Rhythm: Moving Meditation

DANCE, NOT JUST AS a form of entertainment, but as a moving meditation where your body becomes an instrument expressing the rhythm of your soul. Picture it as a joyous celebration where each movement is a step closer to self-discovery.

Play music that resonates with you, close your eyes, and let your body move freely. Dance to the rhythm of your breath, the beat of your heart. Feel the sensations in your body as it becomes a vessel for the expression of your innermost self. Dancing to your own rhythm is not a performance; it's a celebration of the unique symphony that is you.

Sound Mind, Sound Body: Holistic Well-Being

THE CONNECTION BETWEEN sound, mind, and body is not a mere correlation; it's an intricate dance where each partner influences the other. Picture it as a harmonious collaboration where the melodies of sound contribute to the symphony of your holistic well-being.

As you continue to explore the serenity of sound, remember that you are not merely a listener; you are an active participant in the grand symphony of life. Whether it's the healing melody, the power of silence, or the exploration of your personalized sound sanctuary, let the vibrations of sound guide you toward a deeper understanding of yourself and the world around you. The journey of sound is a perpetual invitation to dance to the rhythm of your soul and find joy in the symphony of your existence.

Chapter 13: The Art of Mindful Movement: Dancing with Life's Rhythms

Welcome to the graceful exploration of mindful movement, an art form that goes beyond physical exercise to become a dance with the rhythms of life. In this chapter, we'll sway into the world of intentional movement, discovering how each step, each breath, and each gesture can be a celebration of existence. Picture it as a dance where you are both the choreographer and the dancer, crafting a symphony of mindfulness and movement.

Embodied Presence: The Dance of Being

MINDFUL MOVEMENT BEGINS with a profound awareness of your body in the present moment. It's not just about going through the motions; it's about becoming fully present in the dance of being. Picture it as a gentle awakening, where each movement is a step into the richness of now.

To begin, find a quiet space and stand tall. Close your eyes and take a few deep breaths. Feel the connection of your feet with the ground, the subtle sway of your body with each breath. As you open your eyes, let your movements be deliberate, each step an expression of your conscious presence. Embodied presence is not a rigid posture; it's a fluid dance where your body becomes a vessel for mindfulness.

Breath as the Conductor: Harmonizing with the Inhale and Exhale

IN THE DANCE OF MINDFUL movement, the breath assumes the role of a gentle conductor, guiding the rhythm of each movement. Picture it as a duet where your breath and your body move in harmonious synchrony, creating a melody of peace and vitality.

As you move, pay attention to your breath. With each inhale, let your movements expand, reaching towards the sky. With each exhale, let your body soften, grounding into the earth. The breath as the conductor is not a forceful directive; it's an invitation for your movements to flow with the natural cadence of your breath.

Exploring Gentle Yoga: The Poetry of Movement

GENTLE YOGA IS A POETIC exploration of mindful movement, where each pose becomes a stanza in the poetry of your body. Picture it as a conversation between your breath, your muscles, and the subtle melodies of tranquility.

Begin with simple yoga poses. Allow your body to move with ease, honoring its current capabilities. Feel the stretch, the release, and the gentle engagement of your muscles. Gentle yoga is not a competition; it's a tender dialogue with your body, a way to explore the vast landscapes of movement with compassion.

Walking Meditation: Every Step a Prayer

WALKING BECOMES A SACRED journey in the realm of mindful movement, a meditation where every step is a prayer of gratitude and awareness. Picture it as a pilgrimage where the path itself becomes a sacred ground.

Choose a quiet space for walking meditation. As you take each step, feel the connection with the earth beneath you. Be aware of the subtle movements, the lifting of the foot, the shifting of the weight, the placing of each step. Every step is not just a physical act; it's an expression of mindfulness, a dance with the present moment.

Qi Gong: The Dance of Life Energy

QI GONG, AN ANCIENT Chinese practice, is a dance with life energy, a graceful movement where the body's vital force flows like a river. Picture it as an energetic ballet, where each gesture is an invitation for the Qi to dance through the channels of your being.

Explore simple Qi Gong exercises. Let your movements be fluid, guided by the intention to harmonize the flow of energy within you. Feel the gentle sway, the intentional gestures, and the sense of vitality that Qi Gong brings. The dance of life energy is not a mystical ritual; it's a practical way to cultivate balance and vitality in your everyday life.

Intuitive Movement: Listening to the Body's Whispers

YOUR BODY IS A WISE guide in the dance of mindful movement, and intuitive movement is the art of listening to its whispers. Picture it as a spontaneous dance where each movement is a response to the subtle cues of your body.

Close your eyes and let your body move freely. Allow your limbs to stretch, sway, and express themselves without a predefined structure. Tune in to the sensations—the tension, the release, the joy. Intuitive movement is not a performance; it's a celebration of the innate wisdom that resides within your body.

Dance of Gratitude: Expressing Thankfulness through Movement

GRATITUDE FINDS A BEAUTIFUL expression in the dance of mindful movement. Picture it as a joyful celebration where each movement becomes a gesture of appreciation for the gift of mobility and life.

Create a dance of gratitude by moving intentionally, expressing thankfulness with each gesture. As you move, bring to mind the aspects of your body and life that you are grateful for. The dance of gratitude is not a mere physical activity; it's a heartfelt expression that weaves the threads of appreciation into the fabric of your movement.

Mindful Stretching: Nurturing the Body's Flexibility

STRETCHING IS NOT JUST about reaching for physical flexibility; it's a mindful act of nurturing your body's inherent capacity for movement. Picture it as a gentle unfolding, where each stretch is a caress for your muscles and joints.

Incorporate mindful stretching into your routine. Whether it's reaching for the sky, bending forward, or twisting gently, let each stretch be accompanied by conscious breath and awareness. Mindful stretching is not a competition with your body; it's a loving dialogue that fosters flexibility and ease.

Dance of Joy: Celebrating the Gift of Movement

THE PINNACLE OF MINDFUL movement is the dance of joy, a celebration of the sheer delight of being able to move. Picture it as a jubilant expression where every leap, twirl, and sway is a testament to the gift of movement.

Play music that resonates with joy, close your eyes, and let your body move freely. Feel the exhilaration, the freedom, and the pure delight of expressing yourself through movement. The dance of joy is not a performance for an audience; it's a private celebration of the vitality that pulses within you.

As you continue to explore the art of mindful movement, remember that you are not merely moving your body; you are dancing with the rhythms of life. Whether it's the embodied presence, the breath as the conductor, or the dance of joy, let each movement be a conscious step toward a deeper connection with yourself and the world around you. The dance of mindful movement is an ever-unfolding journey where every step is an invitation to savor the richness of the present moment and dance with the symphony of life's rhythms.

Chapter 14: The Radiance of Mindful Eating: Savoring Every Bite

Enter the enchanting world of mindful eating, a practice that transforms each meal into a symphony of flavors, textures, and gratitude. In this chapter, we'll embark on a culinary journey where every bite becomes a mindful exploration, and each meal is an opportunity to nourish both body and soul. Picture it as a feast for the senses, where the radiance of mindful eating illuminates the joy of being present with your food.

The Art of Presence: Bringing Awareness to the Table

MINDFUL EATING BEGINS with the simple yet profound act of being fully present at the table. It's not just about consuming food; it's about savoring the experience of nourishment in its entirety. Picture it as a ritual where each meal is a celebration and each bite is an expression of gratitude.

As you sit down to eat, take a moment to appreciate the colors, aromas, and arrangement of your food. Before you take the first bite, breathe in deeply, allowing the scents to awaken your senses. The art of presence is not a rush to finish a meal; it's a conscious choice to be fully engaged with the culinary experience unfolding before you.

Engaging the Senses: A Feast for the Palate

MINDFUL EATING IS A feast that engages all your senses, turning each meal into a sensory symphony. Picture it as a banquet where the flavors, textures, and aromas converge to create a culinary masterpiece.

As you take the first bite, pay attention to the explosion of flavors on your palate. Notice the interplay of sweet, savory, bitter, and salty notes. Feel the textures—crispy, creamy, and tender. Engage your sense of smell, letting the aromas add another layer to the experience. Engaging the senses is not a hurried task; it's an invitation to savor the richness of each bite.

Gratitude for the Source: Acknowledging the Journey of Your Food

EVERY MORSEL YOU CONSUME has a journey, a story of growth, harvest, and preparation. Mindful eating is an opportunity to express gratitude for the source of your food. Picture it as a connection with the earth, the farmers, and the hands that prepared the meal.

Before you begin eating, take a moment to reflect on the journey of your food. Consider the labor that went into its production, the sun and rain that nurtured its growth, and the hands that brought it to your table. Expressing gratitude for the source is not a mere formality; it's a heartfelt acknowledgment of the interconnectedness of all life.

Conscious Portioning: Nourishing Without Excess

IN THE WORLD OF MINDFUL eating, portioning is a conscious act of nourishing your body without excess. Picture it as a balance where each serving size is a thoughtful contribution to your well-being.

Serve yourself a portion that aligns with your hunger and nutritional needs. Pay attention to the signals your body sends about fullness. Conscious portioning is not about restriction; it's about fostering a healthy relationship with food, where each bite is a mindful choice.

Slow and Savored: Embracing the Joy of Leisurely Meals

THE PACE OF YOUR MEAL matters in the practice of mindful eating. Slow and savored is not just a suggestion; it's an invitation to embrace the joy of leisurely meals. Picture it as a languid dance where each bite is a step in the rhythm of unhurried enjoyment.

As you eat, put your utensils down between bites. Chew slowly, savoring the flavors and textures. Allow the experience to unfold without the rush of time pressing on you. Slow and savored is not a luxury; it's a commitment to relishing the joy that each bite brings.

Mindful Drinking: Sipping with Awareness

BEVERAGES ARE NOT JUST accompaniments to meals; they are an integral part of mindful eating. Picture mindful drinking as a conscious sip, where each drop is a moment of refreshment and awareness.

Whether it is water, teas, or any beverage of your choice, bring mindfulness to each sip. Feel the temperature, taste the nuances, and appreciate the sensation of hydration. Mindful drinking is not a mindless gulp; it's an acknowledgment of the liquid nourishment that complements your meal.

The Power of Gratitude Rituals: Beginning and Ending with Thanks

GRATITUDE RITUALS BOOKEND the mindful eating experience, infusing each meal with a sense of appreciation. Picture them as gentle bookends, marking the beginning and end of your culinary journey.

Before you start eating, take a moment to express gratitude for the meal before you. It could be a silent reflection, a prayer, or simply a moment of thanks. As you finish, express gratitude once again, acknowledging the nourishment your body received. Gratitude rituals are not religious obligations; they're heartfelt acknowledgments of the abundance present in your life.

Listening to Hunger and Fullness: Honoring Your Body's Signals

YOUR BODY COMMUNICATES its needs through hunger and fullness signals. Mindful eating is a practice of listening to these signals and honoring them with respect. Picture it as a dialogue where your body speaks, and you respond with attunement.

Before you eat, check in with your body. Are you genuinely hungry, or is it a response to emotions or external cues? As you eat, pay attention to the cues of fullness. Listen to your body's whispers, and honor them by stopping when you feel satisfied. Listening to hunger and fullness is not a rigid set of rules; it's an ongoing conversation with your body's wisdom.

Cultivating Mindful Food Choices: A Symphony of Nutrition

MINDFUL EATING EXTENDS beyond the act of consuming food; it involves making conscious choices about what you eat. Picture it as a symphony of nutrition where each ingredient contributes to the harmony of your well-being.

When choosing your meals, consider the nutritional value and how the food will nourish your body. Opt for a variety of colorful fruits and vegetables, whole grains, and lean proteins. Cultivating mindful food choices is not about deprivation; it's about choosing foods that support your health and vitality.

Mindful Eating in Social Settings: Navigating with Presence

SHARING MEALS IN SOCIAL settings adds another layer to the practice of mindful eating. Picture it as a dance where you navigate the social landscape with presence and awareness.

In social gatherings, be mindful of your interactions with food. Engage in conversations, savor each bite, and be conscious of the signals your body sends. Mindful eating in social settings is not about isolation; it's about being fully present with both the company and the meal.

Digestive Gratitude: Acknowledging the Miracle of Digestion

THE JOURNEY OF FOOD doesn't end with consumption; it continues with digestion, a miraculous process orchestrated by your body. Picture it as a silent symphony where each digestive enzyme plays a role in breaking down the nutrients.

As you finish your meal, take a moment to acknowledge the miracle of digestion. Express gratitude for your body's ability to extract nourishment from the food you've eaten. Digestive gratitude is not a scientific analysis; it's a humble acknowledgment of the intricate processes that sustain your life.

Reflective Awareness: Integrating Mindful Eating into Daily Life

MINDFUL EATING IS NOT a sporadic practice; it is an integration into your daily life. Reflective awareness is the key—a conscious acknowledgment of how mindful eating enhances your overall well-being. Picture it as a thread woven into the fabric of your existence, connecting each meal to the tapestry of your life.

Take moments throughout the day to reflect on your eating habits. Notice the sensations, emotions, and thoughts associated with each meal. Reflective awareness is not a self-judgment; it's an ongoing exploration of how mindful eating contributes to your vitality and happiness.

As you continue to explore the radiance of mindful eating, remember that each meal is an opportunity to nourish not just your body but your entire being. Whether it's the art of presence, engaging the senses, or cultivating mindful food choices, let each bite be a conscious step toward a deeper connection with the culinary symphony of life. The radiance of mindful eating is an ongoing journey, an exploration that transforms each meal into a delightful adventure of flavors, textures, and gratitude.

Chapter 15: The Sanctuary Within: Nurturing Your Inner Space

Step into the sanctuary within, an exploration of the landscapes of your mind, emotions, and spirit. In this chapter, we'll embark on a journey of self-discovery, delving into the practices that nurture and cultivate a harmonious inner space. Picture it as a sacred garden where each thought, each emotion, and each moment is an opportunity to tend to the flourishing of your inner sanctuary.

The Mind's Garden: Cultivating Positive Thoughts

YOUR MIND IS A FERTILE ground, and the thoughts you plant are the seeds that sprout into the landscape of your reality. Cultivating positive thoughts is not a mere exercise in optimism; it's a conscious choice to shape the mental garden that surrounds you.

Take a moment to observe your thoughts. Are they nourishing or depleting? Intentionally plant seeds of positivity by focusing on affirmations, gratitude, and constructive reflections. Cultivating positive thoughts is not a denial of challenges; it's a commitment to nurturing a resilient mindset that can weather the storms of life.

Emotional Tending: Acknowledging and Embracing Feelings

EMOTIONS ARE THE COLORS that paint the canvas of your inner space. Acknowledging and embracing feelings is not a call to suppress or control; it's an invitation to be present with the spectrum of emotions that flow through you.

When an emotion arises, take a moment to name it. Is it joy, sadness, anger, or peace? Allow yourself to feel without judgment. Embracing feelings is not a sign of weakness; it's a courageous act of self-compassion that fosters emotional well-being.

Mindful Breath: An Anchor in the Present Moment

IN THE SANCTUARY WITHIN, the breath becomes a reliable anchor, a tool that grounds you in the present moment. Mindful breath is not a complex practice; it's a simple yet powerful technique that connects you to the rhythm of life.

Find a quiet space, sit comfortably, and bring your attention to your breath. Feel the inhale and exhale, the rise and fall of your chest. With each breath, let go of tension and distractions. Mindful breath is not an escape from reality; it's a return to the present moment, where the richness of life unfolds.

The Art of Letting Go: Releasing Attachments

IN THE SANCTUARY WITHIN, the art of letting go becomes a transformative practice, a conscious release of attachments that no longer serve your well-being. Letting go is not a dismissal of the past; it's a liberation that creates space for new growth. Remember, if you are constantly looking back over your shoulder, you cannot see the path before you.

Reflect on aspects of your life that may be holding you back, attachments to situations, relationships, or beliefs. With each breath, visualize releasing these attachments. The art of letting go is not a one-time event; it's an ongoing practice of creating space for the unfolding chapters of your life.

Gratitude Journaling: Nourishing the Soul with Thanks

THE ACT OF EXPRESSING gratitude is a nourishing ritual that cultivates a thriving inner space. Gratitude journaling is not an obligation; it's a joyful practice that amplifies the positive aspects of your life.

Take a few minutes each day to write down things you are grateful for. They could be simple moments, relationships, or aspects of you. Gratitude journaling is not a denial of challenges; it's a conscious shift in focus toward the abundance that surrounds you.

Soulful Reflection: Connecting with Your Essence

IN THE SANCTUARY WITHIN, soulful reflection becomes a lantern, a guiding light that illuminates the depths of your essence. Reflecting on your life's purpose and values is not a philosophical exercise; it's a journey into the core of your being.

Set aside time for soulful reflection. Consider your passions, values, and the things that bring you a sense of fulfillment. Soulful reflection is not a one-size-fits-all endeavor; it's a personalized exploration that aligns your actions with the essence of who you are.

Meditation Practices: Cultivating Inner Stillness

MEDITATION IS A CORNERSTONE in the cultivation of your inner sanctuary, a practice that nurtures inner stillness amid life's cacophony. Meditation is not a mystic ritual; it's a practical tool that enhances clarity, focus, and emotional resilience.

Experiment with different meditation techniques. It could be mindfulness meditation, loving-kindness meditation, or guided visualizations. Find a quiet space, sit comfortably, and allow your mind to settle. Meditation is not an escape from reality; it's a conscious choice to create a haven of tranquility within.

Mindful Movement: Integrating Body and Mind

IN THE SANCTUARY WITHIN, mindful movement becomes a dance, a harmonious integration of body and mind. Engage in activities like yoga, tai chi, or simple stretching to foster a sense of unity between your physical and mental selves.

As you move, pay attention to the sensations in your body. Feel the stretch, the rhythm of your breath, and the groundedness of your movements. Mindful movement is not a fitness regimen; it's a holistic practice that enhances your overall well-being.

Digital Detox: Creating Space for Silence

THE CONSTANT INFLUX of information from the digital world can clutter the serenity of your inner sanctuary. A digital detox is not an abandonment of technology; it's a conscious choice to create moments of silence and connection with yourself.

Designate specific times for digital detox, moments when you unplug and embrace the silence. It could be a walk in nature, quiet reading, or simply sitting in stillness. A digital detox is not a rejection of progress; it's a reclaiming of your inner space from the noise of the external world.

Creative Expression: Giving Voice to the Soul

THE SANCTUARY WITHIN thrives on creative expression, a symphony of colors, words, or movements that give voice to the soul. Engage in creative activities like painting, writing, or dancing to foster a sense of liberation and self-discovery.

Allow yourself to create without judgment. The aim is not perfection; it's the joy of expressing your inner world. Creative expression is not reserved for artists; it's a universal language that connects you to the boundless reservoir of your imagination.

Nurturing Relationships: Cultivating a Supportive Community

IN THE SANCTUARY WITHIN, relationships are pillars that support the architecture of your well-being. Cultivate connections with people who uplift, inspire, and encourage your growth. Nurturing relationships are not based on quantity; they're founded on the quality of mutual understanding and support.

Reflect on your relationships. Are they nourishing or depleting? Invest time in connections that bring positivity and growth. Nurturing relationships are not a one-sided effort; they're a reciprocal dance where both parties contribute to each other's well-being.

Nature Connection: Finding Solace in the Outdoors

NATURE IS A BALM FOR the soul, a sanctuary within a sanctuary. Connect with nature regularly, whether it's a walk in the park, a hike in the mountains, or simply sitting under a tree. Nature connection is not an escape from reality; it's a return to the simplicity and beauty of the natural world.

As you spend time outdoors, let go of distractions and be present. Feel the earth beneath your feet, listen to the rustle of leaves, and breathe in the fresh air. Nature connection is not a luxury; it's an essential part of nurturing your inner sanctuary.

Living with Intention: Shaping Your Inner Landscape

IN THE SANCTUARY WITHIN, living with intention is the sculptor's chisel, a conscious shaping of your inner landscape. Living with intention is not a rigid plan; it's a dynamic approach that aligns your actions with your values and aspirations.

Set intentions for your day, your week, or your year. Consider what matters to you and let those priorities guide your choices. Living with intention is not a guarantee against challenges; it's a compass that steers you toward a life aligned with your deepest values.

As you continue to explore the sanctuary within, remember that the journey is both an art and a science. Whether it's cultivating positive thoughts, engaging in mindful breath, or nurturing relationships, let each practice be a brushstroke in the masterpiece of your inner sanctuary. The sanctuary within is not a distant destination; it's a continual exploration, a home you carry within, where the gardens of your mind, emotions, and spirit flourish in the gentle care of your conscious presence.

Chapter 16: The Symphony of Sleep: Nurturing the Soul in Slumber

Enter the ethereal realm of sleep, a sanctuary where body, mind, and spirit dance in the delicate embrace of dreams. In this chapter, we embark on a nocturnal journey, exploring the profound importance of sleep and the rituals that orchestrate a symphony of restful nights. Picture it as a serenade to your well-being, where each night's rest is a melody that nourishes your soul.

Understanding the Sleep Symphony: The Ballet of REM and NREM

THE SLEEP SYMPHONY is a ballet of two main acts, Rapid Eye Movement (REM) and Non-Rapid Eye Movement (NREM) sleep. Picture it as a choreographed dance where your body and mind traverse different stages, each playing a vital role in the overall composition of your sleep.

During REM sleep, your brain is active, and vivid dreams unfold. It's a stage where memory consolidation occurs, and emotions are processed. In NREM sleep, your body repairs and regrows tissues, and energy is restored. Understanding the sleep symphony is not a scientific jargon; it's a glimpse into the intricate dance that rejuvenates your entire being each night.

Creating a Sleep Sanctuary: The Ritual of Bedtime Preparation

YOUR SLEEP ENVIRONMENT sets the stage for the night's performance. Creating a sleep sanctuary is not a lavish indulgence; it's a thoughtful ritual that signals to your body and mind that it's time to unwind.

Dim the lights an hour before bedtime. Engage in calming activities like reading a book, taking a warm bath, or practicing gentle stretches. Creating a sleep sanctuary is not a rushed routine; it's a gradual descent into the serenity of the night.

The Ritual of Unplugging: Dimming the Lights of the Digital World

IN THE MODERN AGE, the glow of digital screens can disrupt the natural rhythm of sleep. The ritual of unplugging is not a rejection of technology; it's a conscious decision to dim the lights of the digital world and allow your mind to transition into a state of tranquility.

An hour before bed, turn off electronic devices. Let go of the constant stream of information and embrace the stillness. The ritual of unplugging is not a disconnection from reality; it's a mindful choice to honor the sanctity of sleep.

Tea Time Tranquility: Sipping Elixirs for Serenity

TEA TIME BEFORE BED is a ritual of tranquility, a sip of elixirs that calm the senses and prepare the body for rest. Choosing herbal teas like chamomile or valerian root is not a mere beverage choice; it's a deliberate selection of elixirs known for their calming properties.

Brew a warm cup of tea and savor each sip. Let the soothing warmth permeate your body. Tea time tranquility is not a rushed act;

it's a gentle ritual that signals to your body that it's time to transition into a state of relaxation.

Journaling Before Bed: Emptying the Mind onto Paper

THE ACT OF JOURNALING before bed is a ritual of release—an opportunity to empty the mind onto paper. Journaling is not a literary pursuit; it's a therapeutic practice that helps declutter the thoughts and emotions that may linger from the day.

Take a few minutes to jot down your thoughts, worries, or gratitudes. Allow the pen to move freely. Journaling before bed is not a documentation of events; it's a cathartic act that clears the mental space for a night of serene slumber.

Breathing Exercises: The Prelude to Sleep

BEFORE THE CURTAINS of sleep descend, engage in breathing exercises, a prelude that calms the nervous system and signals to your body that it's time to embrace the embrace of rest. Breathing exercises are not a complex practice; they're simple techniques that guide you into a state of relaxation.

Lie down comfortably and focus on your breath. Inhale deeply, allowing your belly to rise, and exhale slowly, letting the breath release any tension. Breathing exercises are not a contest of endurance; they're a gentle invitation for your body to surrender to the soothing rhythms of sleep.

Guided Meditation for Sleep: A Lullaby for the Mind

GUIDED MEDITATION FOR sleep is a lullaby for the mind, a soothing narration that guides you into a state of tranquility. Listening to a guided meditation is not a passive act; it's an active participation in the creation of a peaceful mental landscape.

Find a guided meditation that resonates with you. Close your eyes, listen to the gentle words, and allow your mind to follow the guided journey. Guided meditation for sleep is not a temporary escape; it's a deliberate choice to nurture the mind's transition into a state of repose.

The Dance of Comfort: Choosing the Right Sleep Attire

THE ATTIRE YOU CHOOSE for sleep is part of the dance of comfort, a selection that can influence the quality of your rest. Choosing the right sleep attire is not a fashion statement; it's a consideration of fabrics and styles that contribute to a comfortable and undisturbed night's sleep.

Opt for loose, breathable fabrics like cotton or bamboo. Consider the temperature of your sleep environment when choosing sleep attire. The dance of comfort is not a rigid dress code; it's a personal choice that enhances the physical ease of your sleep.

Aligning with Circadian Rhythms: A Symphony of Natural Timekeeping

THE SLEEP SYMPHONY is harmonized with circadian rhythms, the natural timekeeping of your body that regulates sleep-wake cycles. Aligning with circadian rhythms is not a rigid schedule; it's a conscious effort to honor the natural ebb and flow of your body's energy.

Establish a consistent sleep schedule by going to bed and waking up at the same time every day, even on weekends. Exposure to natural light during the day and dimming lights in the evening helps regulate circadian rhythms. Aligning with circadian rhythms is not a restrictive routine; it's a harmonious dance with the innate timekeeping of your body.

Comfortable Sleep Postures: The Ballet of Restful Positions

THE SLEEP SYMPHONY is choreographed with comfortable sleep postures, the ballet of restful positions that support the alignment of your spine and joints. Choosing sleep postures is not a rigid dictate; it's an exploration of positions that enhance your physical well-being.

Experiment with different sleep postures to find what suits you best. For back sleepers, a pillow under the knees can provide support. Side sleepers may benefit from a pillow between the knees. Comfortable sleep postures are not a one-size-fits-all prescription; they're a personalized discovery of what brings ease to your rest.

Embracing Sleep Aids Mindfully: Supplements and Tools for Rest

THE USE OF SLEEP AIDS, whether supplements or tools, is a mindful embrace, an intentional choice to support rest when needed. Embracing sleep aids mindfully is not an escape from addressing sleep hygiene; it's a conscious decision to complement healthy sleep practices.

Consider natural sleep aids like melatonin or valerian root, or use tools like white noise machines or blackout curtains. Embracing sleep aids mindfully is not a reliance on external crutches; it's a temporary support while you work on fostering a holistic approach to restful sleep.

The Ritual of Awakening: Welcoming the Morning Light

AS THE NIGHT'S SYMPHONY concludes, the ritual of awakening begins, a deliberate act of welcoming the morning light into your space. The ritual of awakening is not a rushed start; it's a gradual transition that sets the tone for the day ahead.

Upon waking, open the curtains to let natural light into your room. Engage in gentle stretches or a moment of gratitude for the new day. The ritual of awakening is not a mechanical routine; it's a conscious choice to embrace the dawning light with a sense of renewal.

Reflecting on Dreams: The Afterglow of the Night's Performance

AS THE MORNING LIGHT bathes the room, take a moment to reflect on your dreams, the afterglow of the night's performance. Reflecting on dreams is not an attempt to decipher cryptic messages; it's a contemplative exploration of the subconscious landscapes that unfolded during the night.

Keep a dream journal by your bedside and jot down any recollections. Reflecting on dreams is not a scientific analysis; it's a playful exploration that invites you to marvel at the mystery and creativity of your inner world.

In the symphony of sleep, each night is a unique performance, a dance of dreams, restoration, and renewal. As you embrace the rituals that guide you into the embrace of rest, remember that the nocturnal journey is not just a necessity; it's a celebration of the body's innate wisdom and the soul's quest for serenity. May your nights be filled with the gentle cadence of the sleep symphony, orchestrating a melody of well-being for your body, mind, and spirit.

Chapter 17: The Morning Ritual: A Symphony of Intentions

Wake to the gentle crescendo of a new day, a morning ritual that sets the tone for the symphony of your life. In this chapter, we dive into the art of crafting a morning routine that nourishes your body, ignites your mind, and nurtures your spirit. Picture it as a sunrise for your soul, a daily overture that beckons you to embrace the possibilities and rhythms of the day ahead.

Waking with Gratitude: A Sunbeam for the Soul

AS YOU OPEN YOUR EYES to the dawn, let the first notes of your morning ritual be those of gratitude. Waking with gratitude is not a formality; it's a conscious acknowledgment of the gift of a new day.

Take a moment to express thanks for the simple act of waking up, for the breath in your lungs, and for the opportunity to savor the moments that lie ahead. Waking with gratitude is not a grand gesture; it's a sunbeam for the soul that illuminates the beauty in the ordinary.

Hydration Harmony: Nourishing the Body with Water

IN THE MORNING SYMPHONY, hydration is the refreshing melody that awakens your body. Hydration harmony is not a mundane task; it's a vital step that jumpstarts your metabolism and replenishes the fluids lost during the night.

Begin your day with a glass of room temperature water. Feel the cool cascade as you hydrate your body. Hydration harmony is not a hasty gulp; it's a gentle libation that invites vitality into your being.

Stretching into the Day: A Ballet of Limbering Movements

THE MORNING IS A CANVAS of possibilities, and stretching into the day is a ballet of limbering movements that prepare your body for the movements of life. Stretching is not a rigid routine; it's a dynamic dance that invigorates your muscles and enhances flexibility.

Engage in simple stretches like reaching for the sky, bending to touch your toes, or twisting gently from side to side. Feel the gradual awakening of your body. Stretching into the day is not a competition; it's a celebration of the wonderful symphony your body is capable of creating.

Mindful Morning Shower: A Rainfall of Renewal

THE MORNING SHOWER is a rainfall of renewal, a mindful ritual that cleanses not only the body but also the mind. A mindful morning shower is not a rushed affair; it's a sensory experience that washes away the residue of the night.

Feel the water cascading over your body. Inhale the soothing scents of your soap or shampoo. Let the shower be a moment of mindfulness, a pause to appreciate the simple joy of cleanliness. A mindful morning shower is not a perfunctory task; it's a sensory celebration that revitalizes your senses.

Nourishing Breakfast Symphony: A Feast for

the Day Ahead

BREAKFAST IS THE CRESCENDO of the morning symphony, a nourishing feast that fuels your body and mind. Crafting a nourishing breakfast symphony is not a chore; it's a creative endeavor that combines flavors, textures, and nutrients.

Opt for a balanced meal with a mix of proteins, carbohydrates, and healthy fats. Whether it's a bowl of oatmeal with fruits, a smoothie, or a savory omelet, let your breakfast be a symphony of tastes that propels you into the day with energy and vitality. A nourishing breakfast symphony is not a monotone affair; it's a vibrant melody that harmonizes with your body's needs.

Mindful Moment of Silence: A Prelude to Mental Clarity

IN THE MORNING SYMPHONY, a mindful moment of silence is the prelude to mental clarity—a brief pause before the day's activities commence. A mindful moment of silence is not an empty space; it's a fertile ground for the seeds of focus and intention.

Sit quietly for a few minutes, focusing on your breath. Allow your mind to settle, and let go of any lingering thoughts from the night. A mindful moment of silence is not a meditation marathon; it's a gentle introduction to the mental clarity that will guide your actions throughout the day.

Setting Daily Intentions: Composing the Day's Melody

WITH A CLEAR MIND, set daily intentions, a composing of the day's melody that guides your actions and choices. Setting daily intentions is not a rigid plan; it's a flexible framework that aligns your activities with your goals.

Consider what you hope to achieve or focus on for the day. Whether it's completing a project, fostering positive relationships, or simply maintaining a sense of joy, let your intentions be the compass for your day's journey. Setting daily intentions is not a strict agenda; it's a personalized score that allows for improvisation and spontaneity.

Connection with Nature: A Symphony of the Elements

IN THE MORNING SYMPHONY, connect with nature, a symphony of the elements that grounds you in the beauty of the natural world. Connecting with nature is not a luxury; it's a recognition of the profound impact the outdoors can have on your well-being.

Take a brief stroll, breathe in the fresh air, or simply stand by an open window and feel the breeze. Connecting with nature is not a time-consuming expedition; it's a humble acknowledgment of the earth's rhythms that synchronize with your own.

Expressive Self-Care: The Art of Grooming and Dressing

ENGAGING IN EXPRESSIVE self-care is a movement in the morning symphony, the art of grooming and dressing that honors your body and uplifts your spirit. Expressive self-care is not a vanity project; it's a mindful act that fosters self-respect and confidence.

Take time to groom yourself, savoring the sensation of each stroke or pat. Choose clothing that makes you feel comfortable and empowered. Expressive self-care is not a fashion show; it's a personal celebration of your unique expression in the grand composition of life.

Morning Mindfulness Meditation: A Prelude to Present Living

IN THE MORNING SYMPHONY, mindfulness meditation is a prelude to present living, an intentional practice that cultivates awareness and presence. Morning mindfulness meditation is not a complex endeavor; it's a gentle immersion into the richness of the present moment.

Find a quiet space, sit comfortably, and focus on your breath. Allow thoughts to come and go without judgment. Morning mindfulness meditation is not a marathon of stillness; it's a gradual unfolding into the serenity of the now.

Expressing Affection: Harmonizing Relationships

IN THE MORNING SYMPHONY, expressing affection is a harmonizing of relationships, a melody that strengthens the bonds with those around you. Expressing affection is not a grand gesture; it's a collection of small acts that convey love and appreciation.

Whether it's a hug, a kind word, or a note left for a loved one, let your expressions of affection be sincere and heartfelt. Expressing affection is not a scripted performance; it's a spontaneous sharing of warmth that contributes to the symphony of connection.

Reviewing Your Schedule: Orchestrating the Day's Plan

BEFORE STEPPING INTO the bustling cadence of the day, review your schedule, a moment of orchestrating the day's plan that enhances efficiency and organization. Reviewing your schedule is not a rigid routine; it's a practical step that ensures a harmonious flow of activities.

Check your calendar, prioritize tasks, and set realistic expectations for the day. Reviewing your schedule is not a stress-inducing exercise; it's a proactive approach that empowers you to navigate the day with clarity and purpose.

Commencing with Action: A Spirited Launch into the Day

AS THE MORNING SYMPHONY reaches its zenith, commence with action, a spirited launch into the day's endeavors. Commencing with action is not a hasty sprint; it's a purposeful stride that propels you forward with enthusiasm and determination.

Begin with a task that aligns with your priorities or a small accomplishment that sets a positive tone. Commencing with action is not a race against time; it's an intentional step that contributes to the unfolding symphony of your day.

In the morning ritual, each element is a note in the composition of your life. As you craft your morning symphony, let it be a reflection of your unique rhythm, a melody that resonates with your aspirations, values, and the cadence of your soul. May each morning be a harmonious overture, inviting you to dance with the symphony of possibilities that unfold with the dawn.

Chapter 18: The Power of Pause: Finding Serenity in Daily Stillness

Enter the sanctuary of stillness, a realm where the cacophony of daily life takes a back seat, and the power of pause emerges as a guiding force. In this chapter, we delve into the transformative practice of incorporating pauses into your day, discovering how these moments of quiet can rejuvenate the mind, nurture the spirit, and create a harmonious cadence in the symphony of your life.

Embracing the Art of Pausing: A Symphony of Rest

IN THE TAPESTRY OF your day, the art of pausing is a symphony of rest, a deliberate choice to interrupt the hustle and bustle with moments of stillness. Embracing the art of pausing is not a luxury; it's a recognition that amidst the demands of life, your well-being deserves a moment of respite.

Choose intervals in your day to consciously pause. Whether it's a brief pause between tasks, a moment of reflection before a meeting, or a few minutes of solitude in nature, let the art of pausing become a rhythmic dance in your daily life. Embracing the art of pausing is not a procrastination tactic; it's a strategic move to infuse your day with serenity.

Breathing Into Stillness: The Ebb and Flow of Breath

THE BREATH IS YOUR companion in the journey of stillness, a steady anchor that grounds you in the present moment. Breathing into stillness is not a complex endeavor; it's a return to the fundamental rhythm that sustains life.

Take a moment to sit comfortably, close your eyes, and focus on your breath. Inhale deeply, feeling the expansion of your chest, and exhale slowly, releasing any tension. Breathing into stillness is not a mechanical exercise; it's a gentle surrender to the ebb and flow of your breath, creating a tranquil space within.

Mindful Minute Retreat: A Sojourn into Inner Quietude

IN THE SYMPHONY OF your day, the mindful minute retreat is a sojourn into inner quietude—a brief escapade that recalibrates your mind and spirit. The mindful minute retreat is not an elaborate excursion; it's a conscious decision to step away from the demands of the external world.

Find a quiet corner, close your eyes, and engage in a minute of mindfulness. Let your thoughts come and go without attachment. The mindful minute retreat is not a race against time; it's a deliberate pause that allows you to reconnect with your inner sanctuary.

Observing the Beauty Break: Noticing the World Around You

AMIDST THE RUSH OF responsibilities, the beauty break is a celebration of the world around you, a pause to observe the intricate details that often go unnoticed. Observing the beauty break is not a distraction; it's an invitation to appreciate the richness of your surroundings.

Step outside, whether it's to your backyard, a nearby park, or simply by your window. Notice the colors, textures, and sounds that surround you. The beauty break is not an indulgence; it's a recognition that even in the midst of busyness, there exists a world of beauty waiting to be acknowledged.

Digital Detox: A Pause from the Virtual Symphony

IN THE MODERN ERA, the digital detox is a pause from the virtual symphony—a conscious interruption of the constant stream of information. The digital detox is not a rejection of technology; it's a mindful choice to create space for genuine connection and reflection.

Allocate moments in your day to disconnect from screens. Whether it's turning off your phone during meals, designating tech-free zones in your home, or scheduling brief breaks from social media, the digital detox is not an isolation tactic; it's a reclaiming of your time and attention.

Journaling Journeys: Mapping the Landscape of Your Thoughts

IN THE SANCTUARY OF pause, journaling journeys become a cartography of your thoughts, a deliberate exploration of the inner landscape. Journaling journeys are not a literary pursuit; they're a heartfelt expression that captures the nuances of your emotions and reflections.

Take a few minutes to jot down your thoughts, aspirations, or even a moment of gratitude. The journaling journey is not a mere documentation; it's a form of self-discovery and a testament to the richness of your inner world.

Savoring Slow: A Gastronomic Pause

IN THE HUSTLE OF THE day, savoring slow is a gastronomic pause, a conscious decision to linger over your meals and relish each bite. Savoring slow is not a culinary critique; it's an appreciation for the sensory experience of nourishing your body.

During meals, put away distractions and savor the flavors, textures, and aromas. Chew slowly, allowing your senses to fully engage with the act of eating. Savoring slow is not a gourmet ritual; it's a mindful approach to nourishment that enhances your connection with the food you consume.

Gratitude Walk: A Stroll of Appreciation

IN THE SYMPHONY OF pause, the gratitude walk is a stroll of appreciation, a movement that harmonizes your steps with a mindset of gratitude. The gratitude walk is not a race to cover distance; it's a leisurely journey that invites you to notice the blessings around you.

As you walk, reflect on the things you're grateful for. It could be the warmth of the sun, the rustling of leaves, or the simple joy of movement. The gratitude walk is not an exercise routine; it's a rhythmic expression of thankfulness.

Connecting Conversations: Pauses in Dialogue

IN THE TAPESTRY OF relationships, connecting conversations are adorned with pauses, a recognition that the spaces between words carry their own significance. Connecting conversations are not a monologue; they're a dance of listening, speaking, and the pauses that foster understanding.

When engaged in conversation, allow for moments of silence. Let the pauses be an opportunity for reflection and genuine connection. Connecting conversations are not a script to follow; they're a collaborative exchange where the pauses hold the unspoken threads of understanding.

Inspirational Interlude: Nourishing the Creative Soul

IN THE SANCTUARY OF pause, the inspirational interlude is a nourishment for the creative soul, a deliberate break that fuels your imagination. The inspirational interlude is not a luxury for artists alone; it's a recognition that everyone possesses a creative essence.

Engage in activities that inspire you, whether it's listening to music, flipping through an art book, or taking a moment to gaze at the sky. The inspirational interlude is not an escape from reality; it's a conscious choice to infuse your day with the sparks of creativity.

Reflective Nightcap: A Toast to the Day's Journey

AS THE DAY WINDS DOWN, the reflective nightcap is a toast to the day's journey, a moment to look back with gratitude and introspection. The reflective nightcap is not an audit of achievements; it's a gentle acknowledgment of the experiences that shaped your day.

Before sleep, take a few minutes to reflect on the positive moments, the challenges overcome, and the lessons learned. The reflective nightcap is not a rigorous evaluation; it's a tranquil pause that prepares you for a restful night.

In the grand symphony of life, the power of pause is the restful note that creates harmony. As you weave these pauses into the fabric of your day, may they become a melody that resonates with the rhythm of your heart, bringing serenity, clarity, and a profound sense of connection to the symphony of your existence.

Chapter 19: The Art of Reflective Rituals: Illuminating Your Life's Canvas

Step into the realm of reflective rituals, a sacred space where moments of contemplation become strokes of illumination on the canvas of your life. In this chapter, we explore the transformative power of weaving reflective rituals into the tapestry of your day, creating a rich mosaic that fosters self-discovery, gratitude, and a profound connection to the evolving masterpiece of your existence.

Morning Pages: Scribbling the Prelude to Your Day

AS THE SUN ASCENDS, morning pages unfurl as the prelude to your day, an intimate dialogue between you and the blank page. Morning pages are not a composition; they're a stream of consciousness, a scribbling of thoughts and musings that pave the way for clarity.

Set aside a few minutes each morning to put pen to paper. Write without judgment or the need for coherence. Morning pages are not a calligraphy showcase; they're a cathartic practice that invites your innermost thoughts to dance across the pages, setting a reflective tone for the day.

Gratitude Mapping: Charting the Landscape of Blessings

IN THE SYMPHONY OF reflective rituals, gratitude mapping is a cartography of blessings, a deliberate act of charting the landscape of what fills your heart with thankfulness. Gratitude mapping is not a topography lesson; it's a mindful exploration that shifts your focus from what's lacking to the abundance surrounding you.

Create a visual representation of gratitude, whether through words, images, or symbols. Reflect on the aspects of your life that elicit gratitude. Gratitude mapping is not a GPS route; it's a personalized journey that unveils the treasures nestled within your daily experiences.

Soundtrack of Reflection: Harmonizing Moments with Music

AMIDST THE RHYTHM OF your day, the soundtrack of reflection is a harmonizing of moments with music, a deliberate choice to infuse your environment with melodies that evoke introspection. The soundtrack of reflection is not a concert; it's a curated playlist that becomes the backdrop to your moments of contemplation.

Select music that resonates with your emotional landscape or enhances the mood you seek. The soundtrack of reflection is not a symphony; it's a fusion of auditory elements that deepens your connection to the stories unfolding in your life.

Photographic Pause: Capturing Timeless Moments

IN THE GALLERY OF REFLECTIVE rituals, the photographic pause is a snapshot of timeless moments, a deliberate act of capturing the beauty and significance of everyday occurrences. The photographic pause is not a photo shoot; it's a spontaneous click that freezes a moment in the flow of time.

Equip yourself with a camera or use your smartphone to capture scenes that resonate with you. The photographic pause is not a curated exhibition; it's an authentic collection of images that narrate the visual poetry of your life.

Seasonal Reflections: Communing with Nature's Rhythms

IN THE REFLECTIVE RITUALS repertoire, seasonal reflections are a communion with nature's rhythms, a conscious observation of the changing seasons and their parallels in your life. Seasonal reflections are not a meteorological study; they're a contemplative practice that aligns your experiences with the cyclical patterns of nature.

Set aside moments to observe the shifting seasons. Note how nature transitions, and reflects on the parallel shifts within you. Seasonal reflections are not a calendar update; they're an attunement to the perennial dance of change.

Daily Dialogue with Self: A Monologue of Inner Discovery

IN THE SANCTUARY OF reflective rituals, a daily dialogue with self unfolds, a monologue of inner discovery that invites you to converse with your thoughts, emotions, and aspirations. The daily dialogue with self is not a soliloquy; it's an interactive conversation that reveals the layers of your inner world.

Carve out a quiet space and engage in a reflective conversation with yourself. Ask questions, express concerns, and acknowledge achievements. The daily dialogue with self is not an interrogation; it's a nurturing discourse that fosters self-awareness and understanding.

Sacred Evening Pause: A Closing Act of Gratitude

AS THE CURTAIN DESCENDS on the day, the sacred evening pause emerges, a closing act of gratitude that brings a sense of fulfillment to your waking hours. The sacred evening pause is not a bedtime ritual; it's a reflective moment that casts a warm glow on the canvas of your day.

Before sleep, take a few minutes to express gratitude for the experiences, lessons, and connections of the day. The sacred evening pause is not a religious rite; it's a personal ceremony that concludes your day with a heart full of appreciation.

Bookend Reflections: Commencing and Concluding Your Day

IN THE BOOK OF REFLECTIVE rituals, bookend reflections are the opening and closing chapters, a practice that frames your day with moments of intention and gratitude. Bookend reflections are not literary annotations; they're the rhythmic inhale and exhale that infuse purpose into your daily narrative.

Begin your day with a reflective intention, setting a positive tone for what lies ahead. Conclude your day with a moment of gratitude, acknowledging the gifts and challenges encountered. Bookend reflections are not a literary convention; they're the bookmarks that highlight the significance of each day in the grand narrative of your life.

Digital Detox Sunset: Unplugging for Evening Serenity

IN THE MODERN SERENADE of reflective rituals, the digital detox sunset is a symphony of unplugging, an intentional pause from the virtual world as the day winds down. The digital detox sunset is not a rejection of technology; it's a mindful choice to create a space for quietude and connection.

As the evening approaches, set a specific time to disconnect from screens. Engage in activities that foster relaxation and genuine connection. The digital detox sunset is not a technological rebellion; it's a deliberate act that opens the door to a serene evening.

Bedtime Gratitude Journal: A Lullaby of Thankfulness

IN THE GENTLE LULLABY of reflective rituals, the bedtime gratitude journal is a whisper of thankfulness, a practice that tucks you into sleep with thoughts of appreciation. The bedtime gratitude journal is not a literary masterpiece; it's a heartfelt expression that transforms your last waking moments into a celebration of gratitude.

Keep a journal by your bedside and jot down a few things you're grateful for each night. The bedtime gratitude journal is not a nightly obligation; it's a gentle rhythm that cradles your consciousness with the warmth of gratitude.

In the palette of reflective rituals, each stroke of intention, gratitude, and contemplation adds depth and vibrancy to the canvas of your life. As you weave these rituals into the fabric of your day, may they become the colors that illuminate your journey, creating a masterpiece that reflects the richness and beauty of your existence.

Chapter 20: The Symphony of Self-Discovery: Unveiling the Melody Within

Enter the crescendo of self-discovery, a symphony that echoes the depths of your being and unravels the melody within. In this final chapter, we embark on a journey of introspection, exploring the transformative power of self-discovery as the grand finale to the book of your life.

Embracing Your Uniqueness: The Overture to Self-Discovery

AS YOU STEP ONTO THE stage of self-discovery, let the overture be the embrace of your uniqueness, a celebration of the individual notes and rhythms that compose the symphony of your essence. Embracing your uniqueness is not a comparison game; it is a recognition that you are an extraordinary composition, irreplicable in the grand tapestry of existence.

Reflect on your strengths, quirks, and the qualities that set you apart. Embracing your uniqueness is not an exercise in arrogance; it's a loving acknowledgment of the distinct melody only you can play in the universal symphony.

Unraveling Layers: A Sonata of Inner Exploration

IN THE SONATA OF SELF-discovery, unraveling layers becomes a poignant movement, a journey of inner exploration that delves into the depths of your thoughts, emotions, and beliefs. Unraveling layers is not a hasty unwrapping; it's a patient peeling back of the intricate veils that shroud your authentic self.

Ask yourself probing questions. What are your core values? What passions ignite your soul? What fears lurk in the shadows? Unraveling layers is not an interrogation; it's an intimate conversation with the various facets of your being, uncovering the treasures hidden within.

Exploring Life's Melodies: A Concerto of Experiences

AS YOU NAVIGATE THE concerto of self-discovery, exploring life's melodies is a harmonious movement, a conscious engagement with the diverse experiences that shape your narrative. Exploring life's melodies is not a spectator sport; it's an active participation in the ever-evolving composition of your journey.

Step out of your comfort zone, embrace new challenges, and savor the sweet harmonies of success and the lessons embedded in setbacks. Exploring life's melodies is not a checklist; it's an immersive dance with the unpredictable rhythms of existence.

Connecting with Your Core: The Ballad of Authenticity

IN THE BALLAD OF SELF-discovery, connecting with your core is a soulful refrain, a commitment to live in alignment with your authentic self. Connecting with your core is not a mask to wear; it's a conscious choice to peel away the layers of societal expectations and reveal the true essence that resides within.

Consider what truly matters to you. What brings you joy? What are your heartfelt aspirations? Connecting with your core is not a popularity contest; it's an intimate dance with your own truth, allowing the melody of authenticity to resound.

Nurturing Compassion: A Lullaby for the Soul

IN THE LULLABY OF SELF-discovery, nurturing compassion is a soothing melody, a gentle lullaby for the soul that encourages kindness toward yourself and others. Nurturing compassion is not a grand gesture; it's a series of small, heartfelt notes that create a harmonious atmosphere.

Practice self-compassion in moments of challenge. Extend understanding and empathy to those around you. Nurturing compassion is not a weakness; it's a strength that fosters connections and infuses your symphony with the warmth of benevolence.

Harvesting Lessons from Dissonance: The Jazz of Resilience

AS YOU NAVIGATE THE jazz of self-discovery, harvesting lessons from dissonance is a resilient improvisation, a recognition that even moments of discord can contribute to the richness of your personal composition. Harvesting lessons from dissonance is not a plea for hardship; it's a mindset that transforms challenges into opportunities for growth.

When faced with difficulties, reflect on the lessons they carry. How can you emerge stronger and wiser? Harvesting lessons from dissonance is not a negation of pain; it's a courageous acknowledgment that every note, whether sweet or sour, adds depth to the melody of your life.

Crafting Your Symphony: A Personalized Composition

IN THE FINALE OF SELF-discovery, crafting your symphony is a personalized composition, a conscious effort to orchestrate your life in alignment with your values, passions, and aspirations. Crafting your symphony is not a rigid score; it's a dynamic, ever-evolving arrangement that adapts to the changing cadence of your journey.

Define your purpose and set meaningful goals. Consider the legacy you wish to leave behind. Crafting your symphony is not a solo performance; it's a collaborative endeavor that weaves your unique melody into the collective tapestry of humanity.

Honoring Your Evolution: The Coda of Growth

AS THE CODA OF SELF-discovery unfolds, honoring your evolution becomes a poignant resolution, a recognition that growth is a constant companion in the melody of life. Honoring your evolution is not a judgment of past choices; it's a gracious acknowledgment that each note played, whether triumphant or melancholic, has contributed to your current composition.

Celebrate your achievements, no matter how small. Embrace the lessons learned from mistakes. Honoring your evolution is not a linear trajectory; it's a cyclical dance of continuous improvement and self-compassion.

Sharing Your Melody: A Symphony of Connection

IN THE GRAND FINALE of self-discovery, sharing your melody is a symphony of connection, a generous offering of your authentic self to the world. Sharing your melody is not a performance for applause; it's a genuine expression that fosters connection and resonance with others.

Share your passions, insights, and vulnerabilities. Be open to the harmonies that emerge when your melody intersects with the tunes of others. Sharing your melody is not a competition; it's a collaborative celebration that enriches the collective symphony of existence.

In the grand symphony of self-discovery, may you find the courage to explore the nuances of your own melody, embrace the ever-changing cadence of growth, and share the beauty of your unique composition with the world. As you become the conductor of your life's orchestra, may the melody within you resound with authenticity, purpose, and the harmonious notes of a life well-lived.

<u>The Beginning</u>

Don't miss out!

Visit the website below and you can sign up to receive emails whenever Richard D. Krause publishes a new book. There's no charge and no obligation.

https://books2read.com/r/B-A-HQUAB-MIYPC

BOOKS 2 READ

Connecting independent readers to independent writers.

Did you love *The Serenity Solution: Mastering Happiness through Meditation*? Then you should read *The Art of Persoal Mastery: A Roadmap to Success and Fulfillment*[1] by Richard D. Krause!

Unlock the Secret to a Life of Success and Profound Fulfillment!

Are you ready to transform your life? To break free from the ordinary and embrace the extraordinary? *"The Art of Personal Mastery: A Roadmap to Success and Fulfillment,"* is your ticket to a world where success is not just measured by external standards, but by the profound fulfillment that resonates deep within your soul.

In this captivating journey, you will discover the timeless philosophy of personal mastery—a philosophy that has guided visionaries, leaders, and seekers throughout history. It's more than self-help; it's the key to becoming the best version of yourself.

---

1. https://books2read.com/u/b6G7Px

2. https://books2read.com/u/b6G7Px

Dive into the core principles of personal mastery, from understanding your unique personality and unlocking your hidden strengths to cultivating self-discipline and resilience. Learn from the wisdom of thought leaders like Peter Senge and witness real-life transformations that will inspire you to embark on your path.

Personal mastery is not a destination; it's a lifelong expedition. It's about aligning your vision, values, and principles with your actions to create a life that's not just successful but profoundly fulfilling. It's about embracing change, overcoming obstacles, and fostering deep connections.

Your masterpiece of life is waiting to be painted. Are you ready to pick up the brush? If you're seeking a roadmap to success, purpose, and a life that resonates with your true self, this book is your guide. Start your journey to personal mastery today and discover the limitless possibilities that await.

"The Art of Personal Mastery: A Roadmap to Success and Fulfillment," is more than a book; it's a call to action, an invitation to transform. Your journey begins here.

Also by Richard D. Krause

The Elderly Trap: Uncovering Scams and Reclaiming Security in the
Golden Years.
Ignite Your Motivation and Achieve Your Dreams
The Art of Persoal Mastery: A Roadmap to Success and Fulfillment
The Serenity Solution: Mastering Happiness through Meditation